Country
Wisdom

I do not think that any civilization can
be called complete until it has progressed
from sophistication to unsophistication,
and made a conscious return to
simplicity of thinking and living.

From *The Importance of Living* by Lin Yutang, 1938

Country Wisdom

David Larkin

A David Larkin Book

Houghton Mifflin Company

Boston   New York   1997

Dedicated to the memory of Ian Ballantine,
a publisher for all seasons

For information about this and other Houghton Mifflin trade and
reference books and multimedia productions, visit The Bookstore at
Houghton Mifflin on the World Wide Web at http://www.hmco.com/trade/.

CIP data is available

Printed in Italy

SFE   10   9   8   7   6   5   4   3   2   1

All "Country Household Hints" and "Country Remedies" are given for
their historical interest and are not recommended by the author for trial.

Contents

Introduction

At one moment, in a village store, I picked up the scent of what has since meant the country to me. I was about three years old, and as I held the hand of a grownup, the smells of apples in bins, sides of bacon, roasted coffee beans in sacks, and wood—perhaps from the sawdust on the plank floor—clung together to make one ambiance. I barely knew what I was smelling then, but over the years, in rural America, France, or Britain, where there are still places that continue to combine these ingredients under one roof, the recognition comes as a true pleasure.

It surprises me that a dim interior is my first country memory, especially as I was an evacuee. I was part of a whole army of children and mothers suddenly uprooted from the industrial Dockland area of east London, expected to be a target of German bombs when war was declared in late summer of 1939.

We had been sent out into the English countryside, and it was very strange. Of course, all my senses were working, and the sheer greenness of it all from my low perspective was wonderful and I was happy, although not sure why my father wasn't with us. Months later, when he did turn up on leave from the army, I was able to tell him the latest of the country wisdom I had learned: what we had here, and not in the smoky East End, was a thing called *spring* — an occasion when all the trees and the ground were covered in blossoms and lots of baby animals and fluffy chicks arrived.

As far as I was concerned the war could go on forever, but I could detect, as young children usually can, that it was hard on the mothers. The British country people, when duty called, had opened their homes, with good grace for the most part. But the forced separation of families, and hosts with different habits, dialects, and standards meant that the situation could not go on for long. So when the attacks did not come often, and with mistaken optimism that the new shelters and defenses would see us through, we trooped back to London. We arrived home just in time for another adventure following the first Battle of Britain—the Blitz. When the air raid sirens started, usually at night, my sister and I were bundled up in the bedclothes and stuffed into the shelter—something like a New England root cellar—that had been dug in our tiny backyard, and most others too. There, fairly snug, and with the smell of earth around us, we listened to the bombs fall feeling absolutely safe. Following the raids there were sites where bombs had done the most awful destruction, but I saw it all as an adventure playground, a new landscape to which nature and my country experiences could return. There is a story that when Noel Coward, the famous playwright and elegant lyricist, was being driven through the devastation, he saw clumps of white flowers—a form of saxifrage—growing through it all. He asked what the flowers were called, and was told that the local name for this cheery weed was "London Pride." He saw this stubborn seed that just waited for disturbed ground to grow as a symbol of the resilience of the people and their ability to survive, and wrote the moving song of the same name. To me, that plant meant an opportunity to see the occasional browsing bee and white butterfly; but better still, the country came into the city in other ways. In the odd, enclosed patches of spare ground and soccer pitches in the Dockland area, wheat was planted and to our little gang it was Kansas, and went on forever. After squeezing through the railings, we made jungle trails and dens. And, amazingly, this wheat brought with it red poppies, red admiral and tortoiseshell butterflies, even a skylark and other songbirds, and rabbits. I remember pounding a handful of wheat kernels with shrapnel on old brick, trying to make flour.

After the war, the country retreated as the cities struggled to rebuild. It was not a happy time. We had to use our initiative to find the country by bus, even if it was to dig potatoes illegally during the mini-famine of 1947. The Boy Scouts were the answer. A farming family in Essex, whom I know to this day, were most kind to our troop of runny-nosed urchins, letting some of us help with the farm work. I think it was then that the countryside recruited me and my strong visual memory came into play. I soon learned which woods burn well on the campfire, that wood ash is the best cleaner for greasy dixies (pots), that stories around the campfire have an ancient potency. If I was lucky, I could get up extra early to help with the milking. I remember once that my enthusiasm was so great that I spent the night in the cowshed bedded down on fresh straw right next to Wendy, an agreeable Jersey, who lent her body heat to me.

I began to hear rhymes about the weather and to find out which wayside plants were useful, like the dock leaf that soothed the stings of the nettles we collected for soup. There were sayings and odd advice, too, which always seemed to have a connection to the truth, with some straight-faced leg-pulling thrown in. I remember the dairyman telling me that I could get rid of the few summer freckles that marched across my nose and cheeks by the application of fresh cow dung. What he didn't know was that I actually liked this seasonal decoration because a couple of girls in school said they looked cute. What we were both sure of, however, was that I half-believed his cure would work.

In the years that followed, even as a young lad in the city, I kept adding to my country wisdom in various ways: I helped my granddad with his vegetables in the back garden, cutting back invasive mint and covering tomatoes and cucumbers, and as I cycled through the English and French countryside on holidays, I began to identify trees, wild herbs, and mushrooms. I also gathered, here and there, more sayings about the weather and nature, and I became acquainted with the writings of Thomas Tusser, the wise 16th-century Essex farmer. When I finally bought a house and several acres in the country, I began to absorb special knowledge about houses, furniture, outbuildings, wells, wood, and so on, while adding to my knowledge of trees, wild plants, weather, lore, and gardening.

Here is my collected country wisdom for all of you who have left the city to work at home as our society restructures itself, for all of you who already have a weekend house or just like exploring the countryside, and for all of you who dream and plan for a house in the country.

From "London Pride"
by Noel Coward

There's a little city flow'r-
ev'ry spring unfailing
Growing in the crevices
by some London railing
Tho' it has a Latin name,
in town and countryside
We in England
call it London Pride.

London Pride has been
handed down to us.
London Pride is a flower
that's free.
London Pride means
our own dear town to us,
And our pride
it for ever will be.

A potato field in eastern England

Moving to the Country

Shortly after I arrived in America, my wife took me on a drive through the countryside of New England. We followed the valleys and hills roughly northward to the end of the Appalachian chain, which runs through western Connecticut, the Berkshire hills of Massachusetts, the Green Mountains of Vermont, and then descends from the New Hampshire mountains into Quebec. Two hours out of Manhattan, when I asked her where the country would start, she said we were already there. It was a pleasant enough ride, often by a river and mostly edged by trees, but I had expected the buildings to gradually dwindle in number and some real space to appear. I was learning the difference between the Old World and the New: Americans prefer to live right on the road, with the space behind their houses. It's a graphic example of a population on the move. Rural Europeans have spent generations moving away from the original track. Their homes are surrounded by trees, and behind walls—and if there's ivy climbing up those walls, so much the better.

The first North American settlers followed the old way. After leaving their coastal stockades, they picked sites that offered the best shelter and a degree of privacy that these independent folk felt they had earned. And they had earned it by using the most important thing they had with them— the axe. Settlers would chop a clearing in the thick forest and erect a fence to stop their livestock from wandering off into the dark green that went on forever. Their buildings were erected with the same tool and the same timber. Although mindful of their space, neighbors always helped one another, starting a tradition of house- and barn-raising that continued as people moved west.

They worked their land roughly in European field patterns. Hedgelike fences were made by rolling together the tough circling roots of the felled trees, and walls were built with stones that emerged everywhere in the disturbed ground. They tried to leave enough trees behind for future use and to hold together the fragile crust of earth resting on glacial rock. They searched for new valleys— bottom land with silt and richer soil—pushing westward towards and through the Appalachians.

When one crosses this range today, things begin to look different. Part of the reason for this is that Thomas Jefferson liked grids. His survey of 1785 started a development that subsequently divided all new United States land into square sections. With such latitude and longitude, straight roads would ease communication and be fair to all new settlers. No longer would city fathers and big landowners, with centralized power emanating from hand-picked sites, dictate the shape of things. Jefferson even dreamt of new towns laid out in grids, furthering the ideals of agrarian equality.

I must confess I don't like the look of the result, only truly visible from the air. To me, it resembles a large piece of bad modern art—thinly painted squares and circles within squares with some rubbing out here and there, unable to completely obscure the subtle original picture underneath.

The benefits and problems of this pattern are here for us to see today. Efficiency of management, harvest, and transportation led to the invention of machinery that only had to go straight, get bigger, and do everything. However, the directions of rivers and streams did not conform to the newly determined shape; some folks got water and floods, others got easily tillable earth, then dust.

Only when this plan ran up against the Rockies later in the 19th century did Americans begin to think about preservation, and then mostly in terms of scenery. Back East, people like Henry David Thoreau, and later, in the West, John Muir, began earnestly to propound the necessity for conservation.

People who move to the country today will live on land that, for the most part, has been experimented on only once. With some knowledge of what went on in their fields, farmhouses, and villages they can adapt to the combination of a new environment and existing history.

A side axe like this was in constant use as land was cleared. After a tree was felled the ax was swung one-handed along the log to make a square post or beam.

Instead of being seen as boundaries, American roads go through farms, exactly as the farmer hoped. The road was a lifeline, a sign of progress. It eased dispatch and delivery, shown by the ramp (just visible behind the first tree on the right), and allowed the folks at home on the left a safe distance from a sometimes muddy farmyard. Of all the outbuildings, the barn, the most important, was usually the farthest from the house and the sparks that might come from the house's chimney.

A Home
in the New World

Here, in what was the heart of the Massachusetts Bay Colony, is a house that is almost three hundred years old. It was built by people who saw terrain such as this as familiar—a wide, flat horizon and salt marshes. They placed it facing south and east, away from the prevailing wind, just as they would have done on the coast of Essex in England. The exterior of the house remains exactly as it was built. With so much good timber growing in the New World, the farmer was able to weatherboard the outside. The planks could be replaced easily when the salt air and rain began to wear the wood. No paint in those days—it was impossibly expensive to get from the old country—and new, bare wood soon changed its color to merge with the rest.

There was plenty of work for new arrivals. Francis Higginson of Salem wrote back to England in 1629: "Of all trades, carpenters are most needfull, therefore bring as many as you can." When they had completed their apprenticeships at the age of twenty-one, many carpenters packed their tool chests and left for the New World, fresh with old ideas. Many early houses were raised by these lads, with the farmer as a helper.

However damp England might have been, the winters here were much colder. Hence the large center chimney with a fireplace opening for every room in the house.

In the near corner is what some have called a coffin door that would have opened directly into a parlor. Owing to the impossibly steep and narrow stairs from the second story, navigation of a coffin out of the house was eased by having the deceased carried down and laid out in the parlor. He or she was then ready to make a dignified exit through this door.

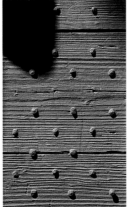

As families moved out of the Plimoth compound onto what was the frontier, sixty miles away, fear of attack prompted them to stud their doors with iron, just as castles were fortified in medieval times.

13

After embarking from the *Mayflower*, the first colonists set themselves up in very much the manner of an East Anglian village, similar to those where many of them had been born. What is missing from this picture is the silhouette of a church tower, a shape that evoked the power of the establishment against which they had protested. In fact, just behind this viewpoint is a reconstruction of a plainly built meeting house for worship, fellowship, and discussion of the plantation's affairs. Much of this picture can still be seen in eastern England today. The wattle fences enclosing the small herd of goats are as common as the supple willow trees that lend their branches to the builder. Behind it a young fruit tree is defended by a triangular hurdle. In the foreground is a hovel that Tusser might have described.

So likewise a hovell will serve for a room,
to stack on the peason, when harvest shall come;
And serve thee in winter moreover than that,
to shut up thy porklings, thou mindest to fat.

When Plimoth Plantation was initially reconstructed, the buildings were erected around stone chimneys. The thinking was that the settlers would have found some use for the rocks that appeared whenever they dug into the ground. Further evidence disproved this sensible theory. The first chimneys had been framed in timber, their insides lined with mud. Thatched roofs, another tradition from Britain, were common at first because the settlers knew that they were light in weight in spite of their bulk, and would last at least sixty years with minimal maintenance. Also, the reeds or flax grew nearby. It was the realization that this climate was drier, making the thatch more flammable, that led to the use of the safer cedar shakes covering the nearest home.

Traditions and Materials

When rural America pushed west, the look of communities changed in subtle ways. Immigrants from different parts of Europe brought with them not only their culture, which would hold them together while they coped with the pre-existing English, French, and Spanish, but also their special language of architecture. Ethnic islands were created on the settlement landscape, and on those islands evidence today shows house and barn shapes, orientations, and architectural details from the Old World.

Houses tend to get smaller the farther they are built from town. Except for large estates, Victorian-, Edwardian-, and Queen Anne-style porches and verandahs tend to be in village or small-town settings. In the mid-1800s, the idea of home as *villa* became popular, and all over rural America plain houses had their appearances changed by decorative elements ordered from catalogues and delivered by railroad car. Eventually, nearly all farm buildings were available this way. Many structures that were shipped by rail are fine historic buildings today.

A sympathetic view of the human impact on the countryside is best explained by wonderful examples of the vernacular language of architecture. Local materials—often just lying around for the taking—are combined with deeply felt traditions borrowed from the past.

The rich farmland of Norfolk and Suffolk yields a continuous harvest of cobbles. It's likely that the stones covering this Victorian cottage were gathered by children who were paid by the owner to fill buckets of cobbles before setting off to school on a spring morning. If one of them was lucky enough to find a stone with a hole all the way through, it would have been pocketed. This was known as a "hag stone," and was believed to be a safeguard against witches. (More on that later.) Common, too, were houses, churches, and walls faced in cobbles that had been split, revealing a flat inside surface that shone like glass.

In Michigan, the same type of round, glacial stones surfaced frequently. Here, larger cobbles are laid from cornerstone to cornerstone in neat rows, first in one direction and then the other. This herringbone pattern, as well as being attractive, actually distributes the weight more evenly. What a prosperous looking farmhouse this is, with its separate chimneys and lovely triangular attic window. It was the pride of Dr. Ticknow, a gentleman farmer and U.S. Navy surgeon, when it was built in 1844.

These sketches show the evolution of a basic American farmhouse. Of course, there are many variations throughout the country, affected by the origin of the settlers, local materials, and other influences. Shown here is what these buildings would have in common.

The early farmhouse is little more than a hovel; first one room, then two, with a mud and timber chimney. The windows are openings, boarded up for warmth. Later, leaded windows with small, diamond-shaped panes were added.

Using the same plan, a timber frame would be raised. Now the house has four rooms, a steep stairway, and a stone or brick center chimney. The doorway and windows are framed, and weatherboarding clads the exterior.

As more room was required, the now-familiar saltbox design evolved.

In the Piedmont and farther west, there is first one structure and then two under one roof. A second floor would be added later. Unlike those in the Northeast, the stone chimneys here are built outside the walls.

This is a dramatic architectural example of a prosperous farm. Ebenezer Wells built a grand addition to his home thirty years after he settled in the heart of New England.

The house at the back was typical of 17th-century dwellings, with its random placement of doors and windows, unpainted exterior, small casement windows, and stone foundation. The building's proportions show a sound construction, which meant safety and comfort to its inhabitants. The new house is a model of symmetry and style, from its brick foundation to its large windows to its clapboards painted robin's-egg blue.

These buildings illustrate the changes that took place on the land over a century and a half. As people such as farmer Wells went about their day-to-day business, America changed, in the words of Captain John Smith, from "a plain wilderness as God first made it," into a successful young nation.

In the Northeast, the basic American farmhouse begins to take shape. With this longer form, there is now room for a front hall and complete separation of the downstairs rooms. A kitchen ell is added, as is a connecting work-shop to the barn and other buildings.

In the Hudson Valley, the Dutch used the same form, but topped their houses with gambrel roofs. The downstairs windows are larger, and have solid shutters. The chimneys are built inside the frame and there are small attic windows. In Pennsylvania, the gable ends, combined with the chimneys, might be of stone.

Later, a porch would be added and new chimneys built for upstairs fireplaces .

Finishing Touches. Now well into the 19th century, dormer windows appear on the raised-seam metal roof. Shutters are added to the large-paned windows. Gingerbread shapes, avail-able from catalogues, adorn the porch and eaves. The chimneys become narrower because the flues for the new, cleaner, iron stoves took up less room.

A mid-19th-century view of how the farmhouse would have looked.

The outbuildings of Stratford Hall, Virginia

The advantages of stone buildings are their great durability; their seldom wanting repairs; their greater security against fire; and their offering to the owners places of abode of greater comfort, both in cold and hot weather. . . It may be thought by many that to erect such a one would be a great undertaking, yet it may be done without either great expense nor much difficulty. Hammered or chisseled stone is adapted to public buildings, or the houses of the wealthy, and is expensive; but comfortable, decent houses may be built with common stone, such as we would use for good field walls. Their happy owners may live freed of that continual intercourse with the paint pot, the lumber yard, and the cut nails of all sizes and dimensions. A stone house substantially put up, will last three hundred years, and will require little or no repairs for the first fifty years.

From *The New England Farmer*
by J.M. Gourgas, January 1828

These stone dwellings last forever, and need few or no repairs, so that money is well invested in them. Their quality does not deteriorate with time, like that of brick or wooden buildings.

From *Our Farm of Two Acres*
by Harriet Martineau, 1865

Next to Ireland, no other country gave up more of its population to the young United States than Norway. In the middle of the 19th century, most Norwegian immigrants went to Wisconsin. This farmhouse was built almost exactly as it would have been "back home." It is simply built, with logs selected for straightness and squared with a broad axe. A good builder could walk along a log and chop a line so straight (see example) that he would not need to go over it again with an adze. Logs were fitted together so neatly that there would be little need to fill in the chinks between them. Another source of pride was the ability to carry on a Norwegian tradition by neatly dovetailing the corners.

The beam cantilevered above the porch not only shows its construction and how the weight was distributed but also shows some prescient wisdom. As the family grew, the right corner was walled in. The near corner would eventually be walled in the same way. And, like most American farmhouses, a porch would be added later. Of all the folk who made a new life in America, perhaps the Norwegians have kept their heritage most intact. The historian Franklin C. Scott wrote: "The Norwegian-Americans have been fortunate in that they have retained a profound love for the fjords and fields of the North while at the same time they have remained conscious of the fact that it was northern nature and economic conditions that impelled them to migrate. They loved their ancestral home in Norway, they took pride in their ancient heritage. Yet they recognized in America the chance for a better life and they appreciated that too."

Near the bottom of our hollow, in the side of a south-facing woody hill, a neighbor is building a very interesting house. After acquiring the land, he set about thinning the trees, sawing the trunks into even lengths that would fit on the andirons of most fireplaces and stacking them to season. Many months later he began, by himself, to build a circular stovewood home. The beauty of this construction is that the fenestration lets in light and solar warmth as the earth moves around the sun. The form is an ancient one, with a chimney in the center for radiation, but with new ideas as well. Following the circular pattern, the logs are laid with their cut ends facing outward. The house is made with a mixture of ash, maple, and oak, trees all found in the hollow.

It's big enough inside so that straight pieces of furniture won't bump against the curved walls. And, by planning ahead, some of the logs project inside or out for storage and other purposes.

Right

A round building avoids the tricky problem of dealing with corners. However, a clever Polish immigrant farmer in Wisconsin stacked squared-off logs at the corners just as a stonemason would. The stovewood method is also found in Quebec and northern Michigan.

Another use of local materials—in this case immediate use. Snowdonia, in North Wales, abounds in stone, slate, and nonconformism. Most Welsh farmers who settled in America came from this area, and most of them could not speak English. Here is The Ugly House in Ty Hyll. It is said to have been built in a day and a night in order for the owner to establish freehold rights to the house and its land. Now mature and charming, the owners don't want to disappoint visitors by tidying up its structure.

Historic precedent says the bigger the roof, the older the building. The saltbox house typifies the shape of historic New England, though the form originated in medieval times. The steeply pitched roof, designed to shed water, resembed the lid of an old-fashioned saltbox when the

rear roof was extended. The addition below the extension was sometimes built of stone. A pleasing feature of some saltbox houses is the slight inward curve of the upper roof as the two sets of timbers meet. The other distinctive shape of this style is the enormous chimney that coped with the fireplaces in each room. Nearer the coast, shingles often covered the walls most exposed to sun and rain. This house in Suffolk County, New York, is—apart from the shingles—almost exactly like the one I was evacuated to in Suffolk, England. Its interior was extremely dark and, like American saltboxes, had small windows. On rainy washdays, clotheshorses in the attic took advantage of the heat that rose through an open trap door to dry the laundry.

Of all the simple house styles, this one defies additional decoration, but—I'm sad to say—not imitation. New saltboxes are dotted here and there in developments, *sans* chimney, completely missing the point of how the building evolved. "Architects" have even designed skylights into the saltbox lids.

Center chimneys needed a lot of thought in their design. The fireplaces they served faced in different directions —sometimes diagonal to each other. Looking at this 1750 Rhode Island chimney, we can see the skilled masonry of the structure-within-a-structure.

Thrifty New Englanders did not waste chimney smoke. Apart from the soot collected to make paint and fertilizer, smoke was used to cure meat. An opening could be made in the chimney as it passed through the attic, and sides of bacon, hams, and sausages would be hung there to be dried and preserved by the smoke.

Space was tight behind the front door of a New England center-chimney home.

The practical and economy-minded Shakers in Maine cover their buildings with what serves best: the side with the worst weather is shingled and creates a bold contrast to the painted clapboards. See how neatly the 1824 Sabbathday Lake Herb House rests on its shaped-stone foundation.

There are many unanswered questions about how the shape of some houses in rural America came to be, especially where people from different countries mingled.

As far as I know, building with logs was not part of the Scotch-Irish history. But as they moved south and then through the Appalachians, they learned the skill from other Protestant folk, such as the Scandinavians and Germans, who were already in Pennsylvania. As they moved west and south, they took the log-building method with them. This is a Tennessee dogtrot house. The dogtrot is the open space between the two evenly sized structures, or cribs, under a common roof. I was impressed with how well this building worked. It allowed for cool breezes in the summer, and the separation of both floors allowed for some privacy. The upstairs

The center of a dogtrot barn in the farmyard.

A look through to the kitchen section of the dogtrot shows its advantages—at least in summer.

landing between the two floors served as a sleeping area on hot nights. Nearly all the family chores could be done in open space, yet under cover. The main room on the left, where the parents also slept, connects to an added kitchen structure behind it. On the right is the parlor, and above are separate rooms for boys and girls. Looking out from the open landing, I could see that the other farm structures were built in the same way, with open space between cribs.

Possible origins. A preserved, 18th-century dogtrot structure in Oslo. I have seen many historic structures like this in Norway, Sweden, and Denmark, often with sod-covered roofs. Settlers in North America remembered this method and used it in the almost treeless High Plains. The edges of the roof are protected by rot-resistant birch bark.

I have never been able to reconcile George Washington's reputation for honesty and the facade of Mount Vernon. The Palladian improvements and enlargements to his farmhouse were finished off with rusticated wooden boards, scored and patterned to make the house appear as though it was built of marble. The style, borrowed from classic Roman architecture, was the latest thing in England before the Revolution. It became very popular on the East Coast of America, but with a difference: the exterior doorways, columns, and arches were frequently made of wood.

Country Interiors

The stark beauty of many American historic rural buildings remains, in my opinion, because there was no original "architect" involved. It is truly folk architecture. There are few plans or drawings. In fact, this prompted the Roosevelt administration to pioneer the Historic American Building Survey in the 1930s. Unemployed trainee architects and students measured and drew threatened farmhouses, barns, mills, churches—all sorts of structures—inside and out. What they learned by doing these fine drawings was how the buildings worked, how they grew, what changes were made, and, in the case of farmhouses and their dependencies, which parts were used and why.

After studying those drawings, I've gained a deeper understanding of the many places I've visited. Over the last ten or so years, I've clambered over many structures, that illustrate in their details the wisdom of the rural

men and women. Yes, these places are mostly restored historic farms, and their clocks have stopped. But I encourage you to think of the interiors as genre paintings without the people; imagine these homes with inhabitants, sometimes full of talk and laughter, sometimes miserable, and nearly always working hard at something.

Although I've spent some time trying to save old farm buildings, it's useless to resurrect these vanished scenes as blueprints for living wisely in the country today. Things have changed too much. But there is much here that we can borrow from the past, not only through my factual descriptions, but also by seeing what the light and colors were like; how unpainted and worn objects have a quality that cannot be faked, their form and function being one; that prized possessions, if only just one or two, are placed with care, out of danger, but in full view.

In the American Southwest, the Spanish built with adobe, a method originally brought to them by the invading Moors from North Africa. The very earth where the house stood supplied the mud bricks, mixed with finely shredded straw and dried in the sun. They were laid, from the ground up, like any bricks, with the same muddy mixture used both as mortar and coating for the finished wall. Coating was done by Native American and Hispanic women, originators of the soft-sculpted angles and smooth finishes on the best historic structures in New Mexico.

An adobe building is easy to live with, if you provide minimum care. Attending to its flat roof and the occasional crack on the surface is easy, and the material is at your feet. My friends with adobe houses enjoy doing this because they feel connected to the earth.

The first Hispanic settlers to move up the Rio Grande did not merge with the native population. They were both missionaries and overlords, and the look of their farms, or haciendas, reflects a defensive style. There were thick outside walls for protection against the attacks of unwilling converts, as well as the unrelenting sun. Inside, everything faced a cloistered courtyard, which gave light to the rooms surrounding the quadrangle. The entire structure, called a *ribat*, originated in the Muslim world. This view of the courtyard of the Martinez Hacienda near Taos, shows the well safely inside, and a ladder to provide access to the roof above the entrance.

As is customary when working with adobe, the shapes in this kitchen evolved as trial and error gradually worked out the best size and positions for both cooking hearth and fireplace. Just like kitchens in the East, the first ones in the Southwest had earthen floors, but in the drier climate they were easier to maintain. After being pounded flat, floors were made smooth by continuous wear. Sometimes ox blood was mixed into the mud to provide a harder finish, but the surface was still porous. Periodically, after absorbing large amounts of bacteria from normal living, the floor would have to be dug up. The dirt was valuable, so nitrous that it could be used for the manufacture of gunpowder.

A rough Plimoth room is illuminated from three sources. The open window on the left, which had no glass, would be covered with oiled parchment or linen in cold weather to let in some light. At night, an inside shutter would be pulled across the opening. Past the open doorway in the center, the light in the fireplace comes from a smoke hole in the roof, which could be shuttered by pulling on a rope on the rare occasions when there was no fire. The rocklike background of the hearth is baked mud, and, as you can see, the timber framing holds it all together. The only protection from the inevitable smoke would be a blanket strung across the hearth.

This room measures roughly sixteen feet deep. Colonial builders used such a span because it was a common measurement in England, based on the area needed to accommodate two teams of oxen. This space, called a bay, would then be halved, such as this interior. Thus, areas divisible by eight became common. Like many others, this structure was overbuilt. Builders brought the European tradition of timber framing with them, so they were adept at making heavy, short lengths do all the framing. It would take time before the colonists took advantage of the plentiful straight, tall, and slim trees.

A Vermeer-like interior illustrates how prosperity came to some farmers in the 17th century. Everything is sturdily built, with all angles supporting each other. The legs of the table, bench, and chair are joined by substantial stretchers that hold them in tension. Early colonial furniture was built for heavy use, with oak the first choice of wood; it would have been knocked around below decks on its voyage from England, and then on a bumpy cart ride to a final destination. It's likely that the table would have traveled in pieces. It would have been rejoined with its wooden pegs, and its top would have rested on the frame. Cloth coverings were common, if affordable, and kept further knocks and scratches from damaging the simply waxed and stained surfaces. This arrangement became very popular again about a hundred years ago. My grandmother's best room always had velvet and tasselled covers on the flat surfaces.

The window glass is set in diamond-shaped mullions because flat glass could only be cut in small pieces in those days. Molten glass was spun out like a big, round, flat lollipop and then cut into shapes. Like the lollipop, it was thicker in the center—which was also the most distorted portion and bought only by the less well-off. Today, ironically, the piece that looks like the bottom of a bottle is the most sought after.

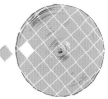

33

For a long time, until habits and fashions were changed by technology, the master bedroom remained downstairs. Once there were separate rooms downstairs, going upstairs, to what was known as a chamber, was for the rest of the family, or guests. After all, it was cold up there. Those upstairs might have had the benefit of a copper warming pan, which, depending on the part of the country, might be given a comic or bawdy name. This picture shows a change of both heart and times: competing with the bed for pride of place is the chest-on-chest, a valuable possession. The clean, woman's shift and man's shirt are ready for the morning. There was little closet space in the 18th-century house.

What we now call the bed would have been known as a bedstead. The bed itself was a tick, or cloth case, stuffed with feathers, which lay upon a mattress filled with coarser material, such as straw, hay, or hair. This, in turn, rested on ropes strung across the bedstead frame. As I was reminded as a child, you were kept warm in bed by what was underneath; what you piled on top made little difference.

The beautifully worked coverlet is pieced callimanco, or glazed wool. During the day, it is likely that it would have been folded back for cleanliness and to prevent the colors from fading. If this couple had been more prosperous they would have used a bed round, a carpet that went around three sides of the bed and saved the paint work on the floor.

Progress was measured differently in northern Virginia. Away from the rich tidewater lands of the south and east the going was tougher, as this interior reflects. The young homesteader, not being able to afford slaves, would have constructed this dwelling by his own labor. It was built with manageable, untrimmed young logs and local stone. The large gaps between logs were fitted with a mixture of earth and straw. It is just one room, with a sleeping loft reached by a ladder. You can see bedding peeking through the split logs, and every other possession is in view.

Not all farms were seen as a sole occupation. The Oliver Kelley Farm, on the banks of the Mississippi in Elk River, Minnesota, is famous for what its owner did as an absentee. After enduring pioneering first years and a winter with little more than wild rice to eat, Kelley eventually became a government clerk in Washington, D.C., for the Department of Agriculture, and then for the U.S. Postal Service. Keeping the farm back home, he began to organize fellow farmers into a countywide society to pool their knowledge and experiences to become more prosperous and secure. There was little interest in Washington, but his ideas took hold in Minnesota, where the organization became popularly known as the Grange. Farmers could cooperate in the buying of equipment and the selling of the harvest. Today, the nationwide organization continues to advocate on farmers' behalf.

Meanwhile, the Kelley farm was run by his wife, with her two daughters. Like many other women, she played an active role in making a go of it. Note the wooden stair leading down from what was the kitchen, or back, door, to the lean-to, or storage space. If there was more work than the family could handle, this area was the best accommodation they could offer to a hired laborer, who, soon after gathering the fall crops, would pack the trunk near the end of the bed and leave for somewhere warmer. The lean-to had a dirt floor and no insulation. The stove would not be enough to cope with the Minnesota cold.

The root cellar under the house might have been less drafty than the laborer's quarters. It was a modern convenience, directly accessible from the kitchen by inside stairs, unlike the earlier root cellars of New England. The bins could store enough potatoes, beets, and carrots to last well into the following year. They would be placed with care in these bins, between layers of earth to protect them from bruising, rotting and to maintain a constant cool temperature. In the 19th century, pumpkins were mostly grown as cattle feed. These were piled inside to avoid frost damage.

So far we have not seen any carpets or polished and waxed floors. In 1840 in Virginia, farming people would be very happy to walk on fine boards such as these. Considering their heavy use, they were well looked after, frequently swept, and occasionally scrubbed. At least once a year the walls and ceilings would be whitewashed, helping to brighten and sanitize the rooms. There was a difference between the whitewash used inside and out. For inside use, the powdered lime would be mixed with size to prevent it from flaking. But size melts when it gets wet, so it would be useless in the rain. For outside use oil was added to the mixture, which made it waterproof.

The bright, checkerboard-like covering on the floor is what we used to call an oilcloth. A piece of canvas was covered with coats of paint and placed in the area where there was the most traffic. In this case, it is in the middle of the room, where the table would be placed when the family settled down to eat.

Back in the north of Ireland, as late as the turn of the century, things changed slowly. Although there was a window with glass and enough crockery for a large family, life was hard. This was open-plan living, with the best bed tucked under the outshot on the right. A linen cloth above the bed protected it from falling dirt. The use of this bed depended on the circumstance, as the farmer and his wife would give it up for an elderly parent or a sick child. The rest of the family would make do on pallets in front of the hearth, on the settle bed, or in the only other room, which was unheated. All the attention in this one-story building was on the fireplace, built with the best stone and the most care. This was where life was focused. In France, family problems were discussed around the dinner table, sometimes in America, too. In England, such discussions took place at the breakfast table. But in Ireland, at night, the place for talk was the fireside. Those "creepie" stools in the semicircle remained in place most of the time. My Irish relatives used a big trestle table for meals and work, then put it away. Staring into the embers, thoughts were collected and conversation made easy without confrontation.

We have a neighboring farmhouse down the hill. It's a crop and dairy farm that keeps going by using every bit of decent land available and by renting good fields and bottom land within a three-mile radius to supply food for the livestock. The farmhouse is white. It has a porch like this one, and the only time we've seen Leo, the farmer, sitting on it was once when it was pouring rain. Though farmers like rain more than most people, he looked as if he wanted it to stop so he could get moving.

We can see how well-positioned everything is, but also the wear and tear. Although both porch roof and floor generally slope downwards to shed water, there was some dampness affecting the bottom of the posts here. The neat solution was to saw off the offending base and use brackets for support. Past the boot scraper are iron lamp holders to lead people along the boardwalk to the gate in the picket fence. Incidentally, *picket* comes from the French *piquer,* to pierce.

We are led from the garden gate, up the rose-covered, herb-edged path, and over the threshold, which is today just part of the door frame. In the past, a threshold would have been more noticeably higher, built so that it would retain the grains of wheat, barley, or rye that were whacked out of their ears by a flail wielded by someone inside. Of course, most thrashing (threshing) was done on the barn floor, but historically, cottagers would do some at home, too—enough for gruel, or to fatten that special goose.

A typical barn threshold looked like this. The boards would be slotted between posts, and more could be added. A breeze would help things, and another opening on the opposite wall was better still. As they flailed away, the draft of wind through the barn would help to separate the wheat from the chaff.

Throughout the farmland of Holland, apart from the sails of wind pumps, there is the singular shape of the barnhouse. It is seen in Denmark and Germany, too. Considering the number of folk who emigrated from these countries, it is surprising that the style never caught on in America. There is some evidence that the Dutch in the Hudson Valley started to build this way and then abandoned the practice. Maybe it was all that extra land. The separate Dutch-style houses and barns that remain have many similarities to the linked barnhouse. In Holland, the inside was divided into several bays. The end bay—never more than one-third of the building— was the house itself. The advantages of such a compact arrangement can be seen here: no early-morning muddy walks to the cowshed and privy, and the farm wife could run everyday affairs with these inside doors open.

The Country Kitchen

Our largest room is variously called the dining room, kitchen, or workroom. Whatever its name of the moment, it's where we spend most of our time. It was an important factor when we first looked at our house. A very open room, it is full of both morning and afternoon light. It has a step down into the kitchen area, barn-like posts and beams, and a large, brick, corner fireplace. When it is filled with people and the smells of cooking, it has a wonderful ambiance. Guests are invited to sit at the long table facing the fire, away from the cooking area, but some are very happy to sit with their backs warmed by the fire, watching the kitchen-area activity.

The traditional American farm kitchen was not subject to changes in style or character—it was what it was. The biggest and most important room on the farm, the kitchen was where everything was done. It may have been connected to a dairy, pantry, scullery, backhouse, or even an outside bake oven or smokehouse. From this center, a woman would command and control the day-to-day activities of the farm. The kitchen door was located so that she could monitor what was taking place in the working buildings, as well as oversee the garden, orchard, farmyard animals and poultry, and the approach of visitors. All this was done while preparing meals for the family and farm workers, making butter, cheese, and soap, pumping water, and many other daily tasks.

There was rarely time or inclination to use the parlor for a rest. Both men and women, after long working days outside and in, would just want dinner and bed. Parlors were used for special occasions, celebrations, formal gatherings, weddings, and funerals. When portable harmoniums, radios, and televisions first became available, they were considered worthy of special attention in this room.

Today, though the television still occupies an honored place there, most country people live their daily lives with radios and television sets in the kitchen.

How we envision past country life, and think about what it can teach us, has been colored largely by one man and his business activities. In the years before World War I, Wallace Nutting was a successful commercial photographer—a sort of pictorialist—who arranged and sold many photographic scenes (suitable for framing) of how he visualized colonial life and its interiors. With posed models in period dress and authentic settings crammed with genuine antiques and artifacts, these pretty pictures are full of information—and misinformation. His philosophy was, the more the merrier. The more items he included in the scene, the more valuable the items became. (And he owned most of them.) When the silver he used to make prints was commandeered during the war, he was out of business. Nutting then began to manufacture and sell "period" furniture, instigating yet another colonial revival. The furniture was quite well made, but then he overdid things, even designing and marketing "colonial" office equipment.

As time went by, Nutting's work collected some credibility. As more historic places were opened to the public, his photographs were used as reference by a few curators, and many enthusiasts. His legacy is with us today in the attractive, colorful jumble of furniture and artifacts crammed into country kitchens, as seen frequently in decorating magazines. But the way to the truth is through original historic inventories or probate studies, when estates changed hands. There you'll find that most country people had few possessions, and those that they did have were hung for use, not display.

Fifty years ago,
the following advice
was given:
From
*How to Furnish Old
American Houses*
by Henry L. Williams and
Ottalie K. Williams

The Welsh dresser... can have various numbers and arrangements of cupboards and drawers, and the shelves can be used for the better dishes, arranged to display their color and beauty.

Sink-side counters also provide storage space for pots and pans, and a dough trough drawer might provide a place to keep rarely used equipment while the top serves as a stand for a toaster, waffle iron, teapot, coffee pot, or just growing plants under a window.

Spice chests on a wall are useful for holding modern tins of spices, nutmegs, or any of the numerous small objects used in the kitchen. The top might form a shelf for the kitchen clock which of course should be of an early type, perhaps a shelf clock, and certainly not one in the form of a white-painted teapot trimmed with red roses! As in the early living room, wall boxes of various kinds can be used for decorative purposes, particularly spoon racks, knife and candle boxes. Painted tin trays also combine decorative value with utility.

In almost any of these early rooms you can use one or more pieces of French Provincial furniture, providing it is of the simpler character. The natural wood chairs with rush seats have much the same feeling as the early Colonial ladder backs.

In 1726, Susanna Wright, an English Quaker woman, bought one hundred acres on the east bank of the Susquehanna River in Pennsylvania, where she began to farm. Eventually, the family acquired land on the opposite riverbank, which is how Wright's Ferry Mansion got its name. The simple yet elegant stone farmhouse is typical of Quaker households—floors, walls, and windows bare and immaculately maintained throughout. This picture of the kitchen at work invites one to wonder how everything could operate and still remain sparkling clean. The plain mantel fixed to the fireplace's massive bressummer beam by small brackets is not decorative but practical, used as a shelf for pewter dishes and other objects. The beautifully engineered and engraved brass winch secured to the beam turns the iron spit hidden by the table.

The brassware would have been cleaned by rubbing with salt and vinegar; the pewter would have had its sheen restored with a coat of oil, polished with "whitening" on a soft cloth. Both the brick floor and the wooden tabletop are sealed and protected from water, dirt, and scratches by coats of beeswax, buffed by hand. The baskets were probably scrubbed with lye, followed by a rinse of strong salt water.

Children have been at work in this kitchen, sitting at the table for some pre-Halloween carving. The Scotch-Irish had moved westward to the banks of the Tennessee and Cumberland rivers by 1850, and celebrating this time of year had always been part of their history. Pumpkins were unknown in Ireland where, originally, raw turnips were carved. However, it did not take long for the bigger, softer pumpkin to take over.

In summer, the woven splint seat would be thoroughly soaked in water and the chair would then be hung upside down in the sun to dry. This would make the sagging disappear. The kitchen is an extension of a log house and built in the same rough-and-ready way. The ladder leads to a loft, where winter foodstuff is stored.

As she adjusted to life on the frontier, the farmer's wife tried to make the best of things. Although little could be done to alter appearances, modern conveniences arrived, including the new sash window and its curtains, store-bought pickle barrels, and a fine new pie safe with screened doors, and drawers underneath.

The cookstove, sensibly raised on squared-off timbers, kept the dust from wood ash to a minimum. It would also heat water for the children's hip bath, which would be placed in front of it on cold winter nights.

There have been more inventions to ease kitchen labor than any other area of the home. The three-legged chopping block is one that has remained unchanged for hundreds of years. Made of hardwood and easy to scrub, many have outlasted generations of families.

By 1900, the design of farmhouses and their satellite buildings was affected by the women who were responsible for not only family and domestic matters but also the efficiency of the whole complex. Mail-order manufacturers of buildings, machinery, and hardware paid special attention to their needs and criticisms. In this progressive era, periodicals such as *The American Agriculturist* and *The American Farmer* printed plans contributed by women. These journals published their shared experiences of life on farms all over the country, full of household tips to increase efficiency. The woman operating the kitchen of this Iowa farm divided her work area into thirds: a main kitchen, a back kitchen, and a long connecting pantry. This partitioning allowed for extra shelving and more work surfaces. The fully operational stove is still in use today and demonstrates considerable output and versatility. A labor-saving potato ricer sits on the easy-to-wipe tablecloth. In warm weather, everyone would have appreciated the new screen door, considering the heat generated by the black and silver "Acorn Utility."

For around $20 ($4 extra for a porcelain top) and about $3 for freight, the back kitchen would get a Hoosier cabinet, described as follows:

A Cabinet Makes Your Day's Work Lighter and Shorter.

It is arranged to bring everything you need within a space smaller than your kitchen table.

Sturdily built of well-seasoned oak; sliding top of white porcelain or nickeled metal.

You will have plenty of room for dishes, bowls, and jars in the china closet.

Large sized flour bin on left side has metal sifter.

Sliding top can be pulled out— gives you a space 40" long and 35" wide to do your work on.

Under the sliding top is a cutting board which pulls out with top.

Block for attaching meat chopper on right side of sliding top.

In the bottom are two drawers where you can keep cutlery and many other small things you need in your work in the kitchen.

The large drawer at bottom has metal bread and cake box with sliding metal lid.

Base cupboard has sliding metal shelf and pan rack.

Three-ply bottom base with substantially built framework.

Height 68" Width 40"
Depth 25".
Shipping Weight 220 lbs.

By 1865, German-speaking peoples began to arrive in large numbers. Settling for the most part in the northern and central states, they tended to stick together in their own regional groups. They traveled light, having to sell everything to make the journey.

This is the kitchen of Mathais Schottler's lonely looking farm on page 76. By 1875, the log walls had been plastered over, and it contained a number of new utensils that fit the six plates of the Royal Atlantic stove. Placing the stove in the center of the room, as the Shakers would, made it easier to use and allowed the heat to radiate better. The scuttle of coal under the bench supplied more heat than wood. On a cold washday, the larger linens and clothes would dry upstairs in the attic.

The "best" china displayed on the worn dresser shelves reminds me of an old photograph. A new farmer, his wife, and children are standing outside a sod-and-log house out on the prairie. Beside them is a rocking chair, a grandmother clock, and a bird in a cage. Resting on the seat of the chair is a china vase. The children hold the bridles of a horse and two cows. They all are wearing their Sunday best, their expressions stiff as they wait for the exposure. They look as if they are being evicted. In fact, they were posed by an itinerant photographer so they could send proud evidence to family back home of how well things were going.

The kitchen of Hildene, the Vermont home of Robert Todd Lincoln, shows some of the gadgets invented in the late 19th and early 20th centuries. In the background is a knife cleaner. Stiff bristles inside the drum removed grime and rust from the steel blades as the drum turned. Enameled containers were popular for keeping dried foodstuffs, and their hard coating made washing colanders, pots, and saucepans easier. Electricity had been installed, and the dependable iron stove acquired a smoother profile, when it no longer needed to generate heat for the kitchen. It has a warming compartment with sliding covers and purpose-built tools to operate the plates and doors. With its brass hanging rail, it looks like a forerunner of the much-loved (and expensive) Aga cookers of present-day English country homes.

A modern Aga stove, very much at home among 300-year-old beams.

The Finns ended up working harder at settling Wisconsin than did other Nordic peoples. Most of them were late arrivals in the immigrant boom at the turn of the last century. The only land left for these desperately poor folk was worn-out "cutovers," remaining from a logging boom in the far north of the state. In Finland there had been widespread unemployment, even starvation, for a population firmly under the thumb of czarist Russia. When compulsory military service was imposed on the men, something had to be done. Rather than comply, many left, hoping to pay back the cost of the steamship ticket by succeeding in the New World.

Would-be farmers left a country where only ten percent of the land was tillable and no farm was larger than twenty acres. They did not set their sights high, disciplined in the Old Country to perform even the most dismal jobs. What they brought with them was an incredible spirit of purpose. They had no money to buy land; to get that money, they became miners, stonecutters, and lumberjacks.

The "cutover" land bought by the Finns was covered with stumps, brush, and stones. Beneath was poor soil and barely enough humus to sustain their first crops; but they made a go of it. After building the good new life, a farming family would be able to have a sauna and other things important in Finnish culture, things they only dreamed of before. Their farmhouses grew easily, because they preferred a modular system, adding complete log sections to existing structures.

This is the inside of the Ketola family farmhouse, first raised in Bayfield County around 1894. It shows the advantage of unfinished log walls, which can take any number of nails, hooks, and wooden pegs without changing character. In the harsh Wisconsin winters, Finns moved easily on home-carved skis. If you look closely at the homemade boots beside the dry sink, you'll notice that the pointed toes turn up to fit securely in ski bindings, yet allow the boots to slip free in an accidental fall.

The stove is an example of Victorian over-decoration. The manufacturers, claiming a combination of aesthetics and efficiency, maintained that "the more surfaces there are, the more heat is broadcast."

Below stairs in Louisiana, an enthusiastic cook renovated this magnificent kitchen of an antebellum plantation house, upriver from New Orleans. Local cypress was employed to make the square table, which is really a work station because of its height and position. We can see the cooking areas of three different periods. The original hearth in the center is now barely filled by the Franklin stove, with a top that serves as a hot plate. On the right is an iron stove for slow cooking and baking, and on the left is a modern countertop with electric burners. The owner had been impressed by the use of niches in the Southwest, and these provide a source of light to the far corners of the kitchen.

The wisdom of country furniture lies in its strength, the use of its materials, and its versatility after years of continuing use. Chests, chairs, tables, beds, and some clever combinations of them all have their stories.

Drawers in old chests were dovetailed in all four corners to slide and stay flush despite changes in humidity. Before a piece left the workshop, the furniture maker would rub a bar of soap along the sides and edges of the drawers so that they would slide even more smoothly.

Country Furniture

I know that the first child born in Plimoth Colony was rocked to sleep aboard the anchored *Mayflower* in a wicker cradle while his father worked to build the first shelters. But probably the earliest piece of furniture to land was a simple lidded chest containing precious worldly goods. It is likely to have been painted in two colors with carving on the front and sides, and with initials—most certainly a wife's, and perhaps her husband's as well—engraved in the front. This box had a symbolic and legal meaning: it was a dower chest, evidence of a wife's rights in the marriage contract. It qualifies as furniture rather than luggage because the corner posts had been slightly extended to become legs.

Over the years, a bottom drawer or two was added to the dower chest. Hence the habit of the bride-to-be to put things away in those drawers for her future marriage. Eventually the chest became all drawers, and waited for another to be stacked on top. (My mother, who came from a busy family of eleven children, reminded me that her first crib as an infant was a bottom drawer placed on two facing chair seats.) The same early chest sometimes opened in the front, and later, with shelves above, became a hutch, or dresser. After living with stools and benches, country people were glad to rest their backs and arms on chairs. They weren't fancy, but their shape indicated that someone local had the use of a lathe to turn the legs and supporting stretchers. The trestle, or sawbuck, table was basically a board supported by a standard, or x- shaped trestle. Styles were those the makers remembered from England, but they were constructed with the plentiful native woods.

Using a variety of woods to fit the purpose, and not caring about matching grain and color, has always suited country people. The wood for the bent back of a chair might be different from the wood for the seat, and the legs might come from a young trunk of still another wood of greater strength—the chair would be painted anyway. When there was the surprise of a new wood, it was used to best advantage. For example, the uniquely American tiger maple revealed its wonderful horizontal patterns only after it was sawn for lumber; it was hard to resist making whole pieces of furniture from it.

My favorite pieces of furniture are combinations that conserved limited space and gave protection from cold drafts. The hutch table could be a table and a chest and sometimes a settle. The tabletop, round or square, was held in place by dowels and could be raised to form a solid chair back; the lid of the chest became the seat.

The best country furniture was made by carpenters rather than by cabinetmakers. Over time, woodworking terms from the Old World and the New have changed their meanings slightly. An English joiner was, in America, a carpenter. In England, a cabinetmaker made fancy cabinets. In America, a good carpenter could work on the massive proportions of timber-framed buildings and also—like Shaker brothers—design built-in cupboards and fashion the dovetails of a clock case.

Almost none of the original furniture made for the first cottage rooms is available now, and what still exists is very expensive. Easier to find—and afford—are the old mail-order chairs, tables, and cabinets that replaced the painted items. We have a cherry and maple table with ten matching chairs that my wife's great-grandparents had when they set up a home on the family farm in the late 1870s. It seats from four to twelve comfortably, as it expands in increments of a foot when leaves are added — another form of family planning. Occasionally, we polish the table with a paste wax to protect it from water and other spills. Sometimes, when one of the chair seats needs reweaving, I think we should replace them all, but since I've seen them in antiques shops, I know that replacements are not far away.

There must have been thousands shipped out by Sears, Roebuck & Co. Later farm furniture, sturdily constructed, became chunky, and much of it has a very prominent chestnut or oak grain that I don't like, but flea marketeers love.

Today there are more and more woodworkers throughout the United States making fine country furniture following original patterns. Some furniture kits available, particularly of Shaker pieces, are of very good value.

There has been a halt in the decline in the numbers of Shaker brothers and sisters in the last few years with additions to the community at Sabbathday Lake in Maine. Neither does the spirit of Shaker design fade in or near other Shaker villages as expert woodworkers continue the tradition of making this elegant, simple, and useful furniture. Another group, the Amish, is growing steadily. If you are lucky enough to be within travelling distance of their homes, Amish journeymen carpenters will rebuild or restore your ailing structures. Fine Amish-made furniture is available throughout the East and Midwest. Their designs are refinements of country pieces. Furniture designers, such as Thomas Moser, have distilled these classic American art forms even further into beautiful, spare furniture for contemporary use. In all, awareness of the history of country people and the materials they used is on the increase. Although a Shaker sister said that she did not want to be remembered as a chair, she did know, as Thomas Merton said, that it was made by someone capable of believing that an angel would like to sit in it.

One of Thomas Jefferson's many inventions, this silver candleholder enabled him to continue reading in a favorite chair once natural light had diminished.

This stout old hutch dresser shows signs of continual wear. It tells the story of a German family kitchen so busy that the door's worn fastenings are replaced as work goes on. I have seen reproduction painted furniture with stress marks here and there, but I doubt if the finishers could bring something off as convincing as this.

Historic Deerfield, in Massachusetts, is a fine place to see how village life went on in the 1700s. The curators have avoided the temptation to clutter the interiors. Instead, they have looked at the probate records of property ownership and inventories. This was what the kitchen furnishings looked like on a day in 1725. Leaning on the outside bricks is a peel, used to place and retrieve loaves of bread from the oven in the back. Also shown are a lug pole with three hooks on which to hang the iron pot, a pair of tongs, and a brass kettle, along with a two-pronged fork hanging from the bressummer beam, another knife and fork, two skillets with legs, an adze, an axe, and two sacks of grain.

This upstairs pantry was, by rural standards, very well equipped, with typical wooden plates and bowls stored with an eye for convenience.

Two sets of initials are on display in this Massachusetts chamber. The maker of the big chest probably also painted it—the decorations are inspired doodles showing the use of his own compass and rule. The simple initials of Mistress Katson King balance his efforts on the upper drawer. Resting on the chest, in a place of honor, is a Bible box.

The walls are interesting because they show how things looked before fashions changed. By the 19th century, walls like this would have been plastered and covered with wallpaper. Anyone lucky enough to have them today would most likely leave them like this. The problem with such large boards is that they would be completely spoiled by 20th-century sockets, holes, and wiring. But as they are not load bearing and simply cover the studs, it's easy to move them somewhere else so that they remain untouched. They can be replaced with less precious material.

The multipurpose, scrubbed-pine dresser on a wall opposite the hearth would be the other main focus in the kitchen. With the family crockery on display, it could also be thought of as the picture-and-sculpture gallery. In the north of Ireland, dressers like this would be the home of the local Belleek mugs shown here; each in its proper space, washed and replaced by its owner. The design of the unit evolved as shelf heights were positioned to accommodate various objects.

Below, one drawer would be for knives, forks, and spoons, the other for overflow and a pair of scissors, pencil, papers, and string long enough to be saved. The bottom compartments had many uses in English, Irish, and Welsh dressers. They might even become the home to newly born puppies, kittens, and chicks, and, sometimes the kennel for a retired sheepdog.

When an old cottage is restored and the studs and braces are exposed, some owners cannot resist the temptation to fill in the gaps. Note the horse brasses alternating with china bric-a-brac on the central posts.

The difference between having things on a dresser for display and putting them away neatly after use is illustrated by this smart, glass-fronted kitchen cupboard. The cups hang on hooks in front of plates that can be easily reached.

Beds

Staying as a guest in a country room with a four-poster bed is an attraction for city people and worth a detour for weekenders. Four-posters, however, were not typical in most historic farmhouses. Before the 1800s, nearly everyone slept on a simple frame, strung with rope to support a mattress. After the 1730s, mostly in towns and among well-off landowners, ceilings rose above eight feet in height, and made four-posters popular until about 1835. The four posts were connected at the top by a frame, or tester, from which hung a valance, often matching the pattern of the curtains below. The curtains were an extra measure of draft protection and privacy, making the bed a chamber in itself. I recall a Shaker room where an outside wall next to the bed was covered with a large sheet of linen, hanging neatly from the pegboard, as protection against the winter cold.

Eventually, the ropes were replaced by boards, making it easier to slide a space-saving trundle bed underneath. The Victorians, in their passion to use industrial solutions to solve domestic problems, argued that wood was unhygienic, full of disease-carrying bugs—and gave us the brass bedstead. For a quarter of the price, you could have iron, with brass knobs. Bed curtains in the form of netting were used before the invention of window screens. These were understandably popular on the four-poster, and even the half-tester, in the South. Though Gloucestershire in England is not known for hot, insect-filled nights, a homemade half-tester here is squeezed under the eaves of a cottage, enabling the skylight windows to remain open in the summer.

A neat "turn-up" bedstead rests against a kitchen wall in Massachusetts. Leaning against the head of the bed is a wrench to tighten the frequently sagging ropes. After being inserted through the gap between the rope and the frame's outside, it twisted, and thus tightened, the rope.

As they moved west, pioneers had to make their own rough bedsteads. In the corner of a dirt-floor cabin, a bed-width away from the walls, a stout, forked stick would be driven firmly into the ground. Two poles resting at right angles would be forced into the log walls to give support to rails that would support the sleepers on their bedding filled with hay or moss. It is not surprising that there is little evidence of these beds today.

A cozily curtained four-poster fits into a chamber bedroom.
Underneath the 18th-century linsey-woolsey coverlet is a bolster,
commonly used with separate pillows, to prop up the sleeper and
lessen pulmonary complaints.

Less massive, and with a more open, airy feeling, was the field, or tent, bedstead of the early 1800s, with its arched frame for the canopy. This design was influenced by the sleeping arrangements of officers in the field, although twin beds were rare before 1900.

Country Chairs

A mushroom slat-back chair

An early German side chair with leather seat

An early Pennsylvania bannister-back armchair

A bow-back Windsor armchair

A Shaker side chair

Just like their houses, the earliest furniture for country people was overbuilt—particularly chairs. Massive, solid-backed, throne-like armchairs gradually gave way to bannister- and ladder-back designs that culminated in the very best Windsor and Shaker chairs. Their builders knew that the weakest part of a chair was where the seat and back joined. The Windsors showed a number of variations of the delicately tapering spokes that support a sitter's back. These spokes rose to meet tops that had shapes generally described as bow, loop, comb, fan, and hoop back. Sometimes braces were employed to give further support, producing a fine example of thrust and counterthrust.

The Shakers made their chairs with combined posts and legs. They solved the stress problem by having this seemingly upright design lean back slightly so that weight would be transferred to the base of the rear legs, where wooden ball-and-socket "tilter" feet took the strain as the sitter leaned back. These tilters were held in place by a thin leather thong attached to the inside of the leg. The Shakers invented this design because they found it hard to tolerate the dents that cherry or maple legs would make on their bare, shining, pine floorboards.

Wallace Nutting, knowledgeable about colonial furniture, in his book *American Windsors*, describes a Windsor as "a stock-leg chair, with a spindle back topped by a bent bow or comb. On a good Windsor, lightness, strength, grace, durability and quaintness are all found in an irresistible blend." He goes on to say, "Construction of the Windsor involves many delicate adjustments and could only be made in fine form by specially trained men. For instance, the seat slants backward. The arm rail slants still more. The bow, when bored for the spindles, is very much cut away and will break unless the best wood, carefully worked, is used." A good chair would be made in tension. The maker knew that

extreme stress would be imposed on the components when they were joined. A leg or spindle wedge driven too loosely would not tighten the tenon; one driven too hard would split the leg, arm, or seat. From tension came strength.

Even though many factories produced the same type of chair, Lambert Hitchcock (1795-1852) became associated with painted chairs with a stencilled design because, early on, he made a practice of labeling his chairs. He made a variety of chairs, such as slat-backs, arrow-backs, Boston rockers, and simple armchairs. The generic "Hitchcock" sometimes includes early Sheraton chairs, which were painted in light colors and had handpainted decorations. By 1820, stencils were used on these chairs, and they were painted in darker colors such as black, brown, green, and pumpkin.

Ladder-back (also called slat-back) chairs originated in England, and were being made in this country by the end of the 1600s. It is a simple design, much liked by country craftsmen, with four or five horizontal slats across a high back. Early chairs, often painted, were made with rush, and later splint, seats; the Shakers used woven tape.

The rocking chair, a classic example of American country furniture, dates from the mid-18th century, when rockers were attached to existing chairs. The curved pieces of wood were attached to the chair by a groove cut into the bottom of the chair leg, or by either pegging or bolting the rocker to the outside of the leg. At first, rockers had the same measurement both in the front and the back, but later the back became longer. From the 1850s on, many rockers were constructed of maple, had a natural finish, and were factory made.

A rare bow-back Windsor arm-chair from Maryland. It has a comb extension above the crest rail and bamboo-style legs.

A comb-back Windsor armchair

A Windsor armchair with bamboo-style legs

A Boston rocker

A Hitchcock side chair

An 1870s side chair with cane seat

The first Shaker's chair. Mother Ann Lee, founder of the Shakers, used this Windsor chair when she stayed at Harvard, Massachusetts. You can see that rockers have been added to the legs. It was made before the Shakers began making furniture for their own use and for the "World's People." The comb-back, or stick-back, style of chair got its name from the town of Windsor in the county of Berkshire, England, which was famous for furniture making.

In Ireland, there is always a *curaird* chair placed inside the back door of every farmhouse. It's an invitation for a visitor to come in and pull the chair to the fire. A tradition in the West, a *curaird,* or visit, is informal and always welcome. The value of your visit is that you bring news. When it is time to leave, you put the chair back where it was. As a child, I was told that if you pick up a chair once, you do it twice.

A bannister-back side chair from a 17th-century Connecticut house.

This chair back, with its nicely engraved lettering, is a simpler version of other crested, bannister-back chairs made in northeast Massachusetts. The curved top and the commemoration to Priscilla Capen, the parson's wife, is very much in the style of the local gravestones. The connection of the date to events in her life is not known.

A Country Workplace

Here, in what used to be Shaker country, there is still an awareness of their skills and traditions. All Shaker brothers had trades, and some had two, or even three or four. Everyone took his part in the village business, farming, building, gardening, smithy work, skilled carpentry, and furniture making. They believed in a variety of labor, seeing it as a source of pleasure and satisfaction. A friend of mine, who is an enthusiastic blacksmith, carver, and woodworker, had this Shaker-influenced wall bench made by a local craftsman. My friend is also following their example of a proper home for each tool, and their founder's maxim "that there is no dirt in heaven."

Among the many fine tools visible in this picture some have a particular connection to the buildings and furniture of rural America.

On the extreme left, two augers hang in their racks on the bottom peg rail. An auger drilled the holes for pegs that held the beams and posts of barns and houses together.

At the top of the wooden post and brace is a traveller. This was used by wheelwrights to measure the length of a rounded surface so that a new tire could be fitted.

Just below it and to the right of the beam is a slick that made surfaces flush, as when pegs protruded in post-and-beam construction. To the right of the slick in the same rack are chisels used by carpenters to fashion the mortises for doorlocks.

On the rack slightly above and to the right is a 125-year-old hand drill that a careful woodworker would use to make a nail hole slightly thinner than the nail itself. When the nail was driven home in thick pieces of timber, the extra space stopped the wood from splitting.

In the middle of the picture is an 18th century German goosewing axe that found its way to the New World, and a hand-forged French axe, to its right, to make wooden legs.

To the right and slightly above the plover is the versatile Stanley 55 Plane. It came with fifty-five interchangeable blades so that every planing task could be handled.

Hanging from the post under the bow saw is a long joiner plane. This would be used to level surfaces where two floorboards joined.

The big saw slightly below and far right is a powerful metal-handled dock saw that when properly sharpened would make short work of a thick plank.

What is the Country?

When people look for country life in Europe, they often think of it in a village setting. This has to do with how history has placed the available houses. The continent has been developed and there are few undiscovered spots. So, being part of a huddle of cottages within walking distance of the church, post office, store, and pub is, to many, a choice country location. There is fresh air in the walled and private back garden with herbs planted by the kitchen door, and the opportunity for pleasant walks along well-maintained lanes and public footpaths through farmland. The parlance of real estate brokers in Britain reflects this desire for a scenic but well-behaved and, above all, quiet life in the country. Buyers realize they are going to be part of something new to them, and are prepared to adapt to a community with ways that are hundreds of years old. This is a tentative step, because they are many years away from being thought of as locals.

In rural America it's not quite like this, although the dreams might be similar. There is much more space and the opportunity for seclusion, but you will, by expediency, become part of the community, and adapt to its pace and social life. I have lived for fourteen years in a remote area; my nearest neighbor is more than half a mile away, the post office is two miles away, and the nearest store a farther two. Looking down our hollow, there is a mountain between me and the nearest town—eight miles away if

I climbed it, and twenty-two miles by road. One becomes localized pretty quickly.

There is a village feeling in America. You can find places quite similar to a European village with its green, inn, church, and post office. But, usually, things are not as close together. The post office is our social center, local news station, and the very best weather bureau. The constant stream of visitors, with their years of local weather experience, combined with what they have just heard from each other, forms a consensus of reliable forecasting.

I thoroughly recommend that new arrivals become prejudiced in favor of local know-how and begin to cast off their city ways. For the most part, it is the builder who knows the best plumber, who knows the best electrician, and so on. They all live in the same area and see each other frequently, so trust is important. And country people have their own rhythm; it comes from adapting to the changes that a community based on family farming has gone through. As the number of farms has diminished, folk remaining have learned new skills, and often have more than one job. Sometimes it's difficult to work with their complicated schedules. However, my faith in our local community has always been rewarded. I could not have had better help and advice.

Buying a House

You will probably begin your search for a country home in an area you have heard about or travelled through. Initially, it is exciting to read the small ads and interpret them in a way that confirms your dreams. But real confirmation is in the travel: to experience the time and distance, to get to the country and look at the potential new home. Once you are in the country and actively looking, the horizon expands, so that the adjoining county or even the next state become areas for prospecting. The ad that may have started it all was placed by a broker who wants your phone call. It is unlikely that the property described will conform to your dreams, or that you will buy it, but it will start a relationship with the broker, who has much more to show you. And importantly, you will start to develop your knowledge of the area.

Most country brokers are friendly and give good information about their area. They want to do so because—should you buy a house from them—they will become your neighbors. They don't always know the complete history of every house and farm, or the details of certain things that give the place its character, but they do have ways of finding out for you.

There are exceptions. Some ads, and house descriptions, need real interpretation. Even a straightforward ad like this one has a language all its own.

MASSACHUSETTS 2 1/2-3 story historic, early 1800s homestead. 5BRs. 4 working FPs, lge country kitchen w/woodstove. Formal living & dining rooms, library. Some original paneling. Stairway to attic and connected carriage hse, partial basement. 8 stall horse barn, 3/4 acre pond, 2-car garage. Owner finance possible.

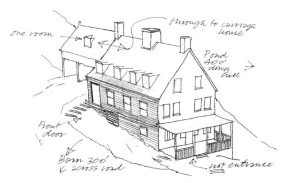

Here is a sketch I've done to show what it actually looked like.

Classified ads can also reveal the personality of the person behind them. Here are a couple of examples that may stretch the truth a little.

SUNNYBROOK CO. I'm lonely. With fresh coat of paint and TLC, I could be a charming 3 BR, 2 bath Cape in unspoiled area w 8 acres of woodls. Minutes from Bedford Falls.

WASHINGTON CO. Architect-designed contemporary with old beams, for woodsy feeling. LR w cathedral ceiling hardwood floors, 3 BR plus master BR w Jacuzzi, large basement/den, eat-in kitchen

Those classified and brochure ads make interesting reading, as we've seen, often revealing more about the advertiser than the property. Here's my personal interpretation of some often-used terms.

colonial- a style. The house could be less than 10 years old, with vinyl siding. Also anything painted white with black shutters.

dead-end road- vehicles will turn around on your property.

historic 1800s Colonial- Colonial America ended in 1783.

lakefront- crowded area.

historic Milton- oldest part of town.

inground pool- 15 ft. tank dug into yard.

minutes- 59 as opposed to 1 hour.

TLC- extensive renovation needed inside and out.

2/3 bedrooms- you could sleep downstairs.

cathedral ceiling- a fancy and inaccurate description of a vaulted roof that may be difficult to heat.

terrific tenants- they are not moving out.

1/2 bath- usually a downstairs toilet and sink.

make an offer- anxious owner.

eat-in kitchen- room to sit down.

great potential- a wreck.

203 K- Federally guaranteed loan to rebuild and make an existing property habitable.

mostly renovated- owner had cash problem.

dirt road- mud, dust, one of the last to be snowplowed, but often where the best places are.

unspoiled- remote.

Tudor style- pieces of wood glued to stucco.

ranch- care needed, often prefabricated, sometimes an ex-mobile home.

bed and breakfast potential- often describes large houses with many bedrooms, few bathrooms and a too-small kitchen.

atrium- any glass roof.

Not so long ago, many British would first open their Sunday papers to the entertainingly honest ads from the broker Roy Brooks. Some people would be so intrigued that they would drive out that very day to confirm his view of the places described. The ads, of course, were enormously successful. Sadly he has passed on, and no one else has had the same touch—or nerve.

NR. ASHFORD. Lge. Tudor hse, former rectory, extremely draughty, badly in need of central heating. Scots owner. Superb example of timberframing. 17c. addition not so well built. Magnificent hall and stone fireplaces, 6 rec, 6 bedrooms, large scullery/dairy. Primitive servants accm. over stables. Rest of outbuilding in dreadful condition. Next to dilapidated church yard—suit BBC type. A treasure. View by appointment only (2 unpleasant dogs.)

WINDSOR. Scruffy stone and red brick Victorian on boring road but with fine views to southwest and castle. Used to be a trio of labourers cottages, now knocked through to form 3/4 bedrooms, 3 recep and V large kitchen. Small dining nook, 3 fireplaces-one good needs sweeping, Interesting garden with 8 hives. Bees left w/ owner.

Could be good. Offers?

Mr. Brooks always sold interesting houses, and the scruffy Victorian would probably have ended up looking like this.

How to Look at a House

Local broker friends offer the following helpful advice:

When looking for a country house, you should expect the broker, over the phone, to tell you the advantages and disadvantages of the property, especially if reaching it requires a long trip. They suggest a buyer see the house at the worst possible time of the year—mud season is good. Then, as you approach the house, look at the roofline first. In a 500-year-old English cottage, a gentle dip in the middle might have charm and indicate both the gradual settling of the beams and how well it was built. Here in the U.S., it could denote serious and expensive structural decline. Look for big trees quite near the house—good for shade, but possibly undermining the foundation, or in need of removal before a storm brings them crashing down. Inside, note which direction the main rooms face and get a feeling for where the sun and natural light fall throughout the day. Originally, much thought would have gone into this, but the present owner might have changed the use of various rooms. Get down into the cellar and up into the attic to check the general state of the structure: plumbing, wiring, and insulation. Another friend, who is involved in saving old buildings, says that he listens to the house—how the old stairway creaks, the noises of wind, the rattle of doors and windows, even the plumbing sounds.

As the law requires, the broker should point out such things as the likely noise of agricultural machinery, that manure may be spread on nearby fields, that there will be dust from farming activity—things which to me, and I hope to you, are taken as part of country life. The racket from the birds' dawn chorus will come as a bonus. Serious potential buyers should inform themselves about the status of the properties surrounding them in order to protect both their privacy and their investment. For example, are there zoning laws that will ensure the look and the value of the area? Is it about to be subdivided? Can a commercial enterprise open across the road? If you love the house and decide to buy it based on what you have learned, you will, of course, want a detailed inspection by a professional.

Location and basic architecture are, to me, the most important factors in buying a country home. Seeing the right house for the first time in that perfect location, of course, is followed by an eagerness to see if the interior supports the favorable first opinion. The typical interior of a family farmhouse will have changed very slowly but steadily. By the time it has been in the hands of the third or fourth generation, the improvements may hide most of the original features. However, if the basic features—the bare bones of the construction, the size of the rooms, the way the windows face, the chimneys and fireplaces—are still intact, any problems are probably aesthetic ones. A typical example follows. A farming couple wish to sell their home and retire elsewhere. It is tight, warm, neat, and clean. The old ceiling, originally beamed then plastered, is covered with the latest in tiles. The old floorboards have been replaced by solid floors in an easy-to-clean material, or, in some places, are covered with wall-to-wall carpeting. The original doors have been replaced by modern ones without panels, and with doorknobs in place of handles. The old living room fireplace has been boarded up, and there are new aluminum thermal windows. This family has spent years getting away from the old-fashioned days, and does not understand why a potential buyer would be foolish enough to deconstruct their careful renovations.

If you do buy your house because of its location and basic architecture, why not live in it as it is for a while? You can restore it in stages, and still get the benefits of country living.

A Shaker window with old glass panes and without curtains shows how light falls on the floor of a dwelling house. This old illustration shows how one slightly larger window brings in more light than two smaller ones. The sun is directly in front of windows for only a small part of the day; it usually enters at a more or less acute angle. Look at what the shadows do. A single three-foot window would deliver more than twice the light of a two foot one. The Shakers also used the old way of angling the openings to let in more light.

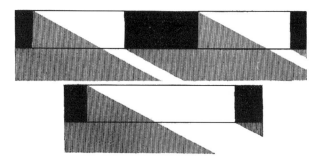

Examining the insides of old roofs is very important, but don't worry too much about smoke-blackened rafters near the chimney. I saw the remains of a 450-year-old barn that had just burned down. The walls and roof had gone, and all that remained were the large frames and braces, the biggest pieces of timber. They looked and smelled as burnt, hosed-down wood does. But the restorer was happy because, in his view, the building was saved. The wood had aged like iron and the acrid coating would deter even the most determined insect.

The 245-year-old lock-raftered roof of the Casey Farm in Rhode Island has had some problems, but is getting better with age.

Inspecting a House

Space

Walk through the house and ask yourself if it has enough rooms. Will it suit your lifestyle, your need for privacy, and your requirements for work space without expensive additions or remodeling? Remember, extra rooms can always be closed off—at no cost—until needed.

Exterior

Stand back from the house and look at it from all corners and sides. Note if the house leans in any particular place, or if the corners are out of line. If so, move closer and look for the cause. It could be the foundation, dry rot in supporting timbers, or termites. If things are just a bit off, keep in mind that it may be due to natural aging, and that many sound houses are not absolutely level.

Check the foundation for cracks. Hairline cracks are not usually serious, but if there are large cracks, the structure may have settled, and may need major work. If you really want the house, bring in a contractor to assess the situation, and make the cost of repair part of your negotiation.

Paint

Wooden houses periodically need repainting, and the side exposed to the harshest weather will need to be painted more often than the others. However, there is a difference between normal wear and paint that is peeling because of moisture either outside or inside the house. Moisture can enter through cracks under the outside boards and then, to get back out, pushes back through the boards and splits and peels the paint. Moisture can also originate inside a house with poor ventilation and poor insulation, especially in the winter. Warm air pushes out to meet the cold air and causes condensation on the inside of the boards. If it is absorbed, the boards will become damp and won't hold paint. Extensive peeling and blistering paint should alert you to a problem that will need to be corrected.

Drainage

Good drainage is very important in maintaining a house. Excess water can weaken the soil beneath the foundation, and excess moisture can cause wood rot and mold underneath the house and in the cellar or basement. If there is a dirt floor, look for heavily cracked earth; if floors and walls are concrete, look for watermarks.

Windows

Check the wood next to glass panes for softness. Cracked putty, which allows water to enter, can lead to fungal growth that rots wood. This can happen also in spots where there isn't enough air circulation to dry moisture. If there is dry rot, the wood will have to be repaired or replaced.

Roofs

A new roof is expensive, so you will want to examine carefully the roof on any house in which you are interested. First, ask the owner its age. Check for water stains on the attic walls or boards and beams. They will show where water either entered in the past, or is coming in currently. Turn out the lights and try to find holes overhead. Tiny holes in wood shingles will probably swell enough when wet to stop leaks, but asphalt or fiberglass will not swell. Holes in asphalt or fiberglass roofs indicate replacement is in order.

If you can get up on the roof safely, look for sources of leaks and holes, and examine the wear, especially on the side that gets the most intense sun exposure. Sun is very damaging to all types of roofs: it dries out composition shingles, eventually destroying the mineral coating, and it dries the oil out of wood shingles, making them brittle.

Many old houses have had one layer of roofing put on top of another for economy. This is important to check because, in snow country, too many layers plus the weight of snow is dangerous and can cause structural damage. You will also want to know if you will have to pay extra for removal of these layers when a new roof is put on.

An example of an effective aluminum roof strip.

In areas with freezing temperatures, heavy snow on the roof may cause ice dams. Heat from the house rises, sometimes through the attic, causing the snow to turn to  ice on the edge of the roof. As heat continues to rise, it melts some of the ice next to the roof. Then, the water trapped by the ice above it is forced under the shingles and into the house. Check for stains on walls and beams inside to see if this has been happening. There are solutions such as more insulation in the attic, electric strips to melt the ice, or aluminum strips along the roof edge.

Electricity

The electrical system of an old house can be dangerous and unpredictable. You will want to have it inspected by a professional, although you can look for obvious signs of problems such as old wiring, new wiring that looks messy, flickering lights, or lack of wall outlets. Some older houses may need new wiring for safety, while others, although safe, may not have enough capacity for all of today's appliances.

Fireplace

Look inside the fireplace to see if the bricks are in good condition. Loose firebricks will need new grout to hold them in, and crumbling or cracked bricks should be replaced by a mason. Next, look up the flue to see if there is a damper, and make certain it operates. If there is no damper, there will be a considerable loss of heat during the winter, and in the summer bats and insects might enter the house.

The lintel is a heavy piece of metal or wood that supports the bricks over the fireplace opening. If there is a wide vertical crack in the lintel, growing thinner as it rises, it could mean that the lintel is weak and starting to sag. Inspect carefully, because replacing it is a difficult operation.

When serious about buying a particular house, ask to start a fire to determine that the draw is good, and that there is no smoking. However, make sure you open the damper first, or the room will be full of smoke.

Check the condition of the outside bricks to see if the mortar needs to be repointed due to erosion caused by the weather. If there are cracks running down the bricks,

it could indicate that the chimney was improperly built, and that, for example, the flue expands against the bricks as it heats.

Plumbing

Check the water pressure in the bathrooms by flushing the toilet, running the shower, and turning on the sink faucets simultaneously. Notice if the force is diminished, which can indicate problems with the water supply or with old plumbing. Also, check the ceilings under all bathrooms for stains that indicate leaks or faulty plumbing. Look in the cellar to see if the plumbing is superior copper, or galvanized steel, which tends to collect rust and mineral deposits.

Water Heaters

It is important to determine the age of the water heater, as they generally last no more than fifteen years. The owner should be able to provide this information. As for capacity, a thirty-gallon tank, heated by gas or oil, is the rule for three people, and forty gallons for four. Electrically heated tanks do not have the same high recovery rate, so larger tanks are required. Some water heaters are part of the furnace, so you can check both at the same time.

Heating

You will want to determine the type of heating system in the house, its age, and state of repair. Following are those most widely used today. Forced-air furnaces, run by either gas or oil, have a motor that pushes heated air through ducts. They are very efficient. Space heaters are located on walls and heat the area around them, but not much more. Electric heat from baseboard elements is clean and quiet but often expensive, depending on the area. Hydronic furnaces pump hot water through baseboard radiators, and also can heat water for the house. Radiant heat is usually installed beneath floors, with hot water pipes either in concrete or between the joists that support wood flooring. In old houses, you may find a still-reliable steam hot-water system connected to radiators; however, replacing the boiler with a new one will save a great deal of fuel, and give you the opportunity to eliminate a separate water heater.

Septic Tanks

In the country, septic tanks with drainage is the normal way to handle sewage. Waste flows into the underground tank where bacteria break down the solids. The waste water flows into a leach field with pipes to distribute it over a large area. A properly maintained system can provide up to twenty years of service, at which time a new tank is probably needed. It is, however, necessary to have the tank pumped out on a regular basis, depending on usage. Ask the seller for the age and location of the tank and the date it was last pumped out.

Environment

Although most old houses are free of environmental hazards, it is advisable to check for those most common, such as asbestos, lead, and radon.

Asbestos, before its dangers were known, was used as insulation, and would most likely be wrapped around ducts and pipes, or in the walls and attic. Pipes wrapped with a substance that looks like plaster, with corrugated material, or with gray material inside canvas could indicate the presence of asbestos. If it is not damaged it can be left alone, but if torn, asbestos fibers are being released. An expert should handle the removal. Find out what insulation has been used in the walls, and ask for a sample for testing if there are any doubts.

Lead may be present either in the plumbing or in old paint. If you find galvanized or plastic pipes, they are probably free of lead. However, if you find copper pipes be aware that, until recently, their fittings were soldered with a mixture containing a high concentration of lead, and you should have the water tested. Lead paint is hazardous when it is sanded or when chips are eaten by children. Though it can be removed by a trained contractor when you remodel, and doors or moldings can be replaced, it could be a costly project.

Radon is a natural, radioactive gas that is released from underground uranium and cannot be detected by the senses. Long exposure to radon can cause lung cancer, so you may want to test for it. If it is detected, there are ways to ventilate your house to prevent radon buildup.

Pests

In general, termites live in warm climates, but even houses in the North may have areas that termites find suitable. It is best to have an inspection to protect your interests. Any termite invasion should be taken care of by professionals and paid for by the owner before you buy the house. Subterranean termites live in the soil but feed on wood, often by building mud tubes up a foundation wall in order to reach house timbers. Mud tubes on exterior foundation walls are clues that they have taken up residence. Check the cellar and crawl spaces to spot any mud tubes there. If you see any, poke the surrounding wood with a pencil or screwdriver; soft wood means the termites have destroyed it. Dry-wood termites need no soil contact and are common in southern coastal areas. They make holes in the wood and discharge pellets that you can look for along baseboards, in attics, and under floors. Damp-wood termites live mostly in decaying or damp wood around decks, bathrooms, or roof rafters. They are found primarily in the Northwest.

Big and black, carpenter ants make large tunnels in wood, but make their nests elsewhere. Their presence can be detected by a fine sawdust around baseboards or posts. Sometimes finding the nest is difficult, but it can be eliminated by pesticides.

Powder-post beetles do major damage to a house and destroy furniture: they turn wood into powder. Wood surfaces are covered with small, round holes made by larvae as they reach adulthood and bore out of the wood. By the time the holes appear, beetles may have been in the house for several years. If you see powder or holes, poke the wood to find out if it has been badly weakened. A professional will be needed to handle the job of getting these pests under control.

Using a Fireplace

Early fall is a good time to get your pile of kindling ready for the winter. Small pieces of kindling wood will ignite quickly and help get your hardwood logs burning. You can walk around your field and pick up dry tree limbs and sticks that can be broken into the right size for the fireplace, or split softwood such as pine into strips.

A few minutes before starting a fire, open the damper to allow the smoke to go up the chimney. Sometimes when a fire first begins, smoke comes back into the room because the chimney is not yet drawing the proper balance between inside and outside air. Next, take a rolled section of newspaper, light one end and hold it directly under the flue to prewarm the walls and start the draw. If there is still smoke, the house may be too airtight, so it may be necessary to crack a window until the fire gets going. Even the best fireplace can get backup puffs on windy days, but if this is a constant problem you might want to add a chimney cap. Also, eliminate any nearby tree that has grown tall enough to block airflow across the chimney, causing backpuffs down the flue. If these measures fail, the chimney may have serious problems that require professional help.

To prepare for the fire, pile the kindling on top of rolled or crumpled newspaper placed towards the back of the fireplace between the andirons. Add two to three pieces of dry hardwood on top, then light the paper. As the fire gets going, use a poker to keep enough space between the logs so there is air for efficient burning.

Once the fire has died out and is no longer smoldering, close the damper. This will stop the warm air in the room from escaping up the chimney, and you will not be paying for fuel to heat the outside. Plan ahead to let the fire burn down completely before you retire, because if you close the damper too soon, the house will fill with smoke.

Fireplace Safety

A fireplace in good condition is extremely important for safety. You must check, when you move in and regularly afterwards, that the mortar on the chimney is not crumbling, the flue has not cracked, and the firebricks are not loose or crumbling. If any of these conditions exist, have them repaired as soon as possible. If you use the fireplace daily, it is equally important to have the chimney cleaned every year, because creosote will accummulate in the flue, and sparks shooting upward can start a fire. Country folk have been known to remove creosote by pulling a small evergreen tree upside down through the chimney. However, most people call in chimney sweeps, who will also point out any problems found during cleaning. Our chimney sweep advised us that there was a build-up of creosote in our chimney as a result of too many slow-burning fires. The way to minimize creosote, he told us, is to have frequent hot, intense-burning fires. Smoldering overnight fires are not a good idea.

One day, in spite of taking all precautions, you may hear an unusual crackling or roaring sound, signalling a chimney fire. Immediately stop the air flow by closing the damper and any ducts, *call the fire department*, and get all family, guests, and pets outside. You should have several fire extinguishers in the house. Use one to douse the original wood fire while waiting for the firefighters. If there is easy access to the roof, you can also try to cut off oxygen outside at the top of the flue with a heavy metal object or cement blocks and, at the same time, check for sparks. The chimney is under terrible pressure and, unless it is extemely well built, the fire can break through into adjoining beams and lathing. If there are signs of this, *leave immediately*. Once the fire is out and the fire chief feels it is safe to return to the house, do not reopen the damper or any ducts for at least twenty-four hours; otherwise, oxygen might set off smoldering bits of wood. Finally, have your fireplace and chimney checked and all the damaged parts repaired or replaced by professionals.

Our own chanterelles

Cookware made of cast iron is extremely durable and an excellent heat conductor. Years ago, it was considered the best available equipment, and even today it is a favorite of many chefs. A good cast-iron pan is heavy and made all in one piece. The bottom and sides should meet in a smooth curve, without a welded seam. One of the best bargains still available for your country kitchen, it's easy to find pots and frying pans of all sizes, as well as griddles, muffin pans, and other cast-iron items at tag sales and ordinary "antiques" stores. On a trip to New Orleans, we were delighted to find, in a back-road shop, a very large frying pan—the perfect size for frying trout from our pond.

To remove rust from your cast-iron cookware, fill with a 50/50 solution of vinegar and water and bring to a boil. After the solution is cool, rub the inside with steel wool, discard the solution, then rinse and dry. Alternately, you can mix sand and vegetable oil, scrub with steel wool, then rinse and dry. To season, coat the rust-free utensils with vegetable or mineral oil, and place in a warm (250°F) oven for an hour. The porous cast iron will absorb most of the oil, and any excess can be removed with paper towels.

The Cooking Fire

Until the arrival of the cast-iron cookstove, almost all cooking was done over an open fire in the kitchen fireplace. A well-established fire was amazingly efficient, allowing the cook to boil water, roast meat on a spit, simmer a stew, and bake pies or breads. Most fireplaces had a crane fastened to the wall that could swing in and out. From this crane hung the adjustable hooked trammel for raising and lowering the pots. Spits for roasting meat ranged from simple iron bars turned by hand, to sophisticated multiple spits turned by a clock-work mechanism. Other equipment included grills and trivets that supported cast-iron pots, griddles, skillets, and Dutch ovens (pots with tight lids that are either concave or turned up at the rim to hold hot coals on top). You can visit historic houses throughout the country, or places like historic Williamsburg, Virginia, Deerfield, Massachusetts, and Greenfield, Michigan, to see fully equipped kitchen fireplaces, and sometimes a demonstration of their use.

Cooking in a fireplace is not difficult to learn. It can be done successfully with patience and only a few basic utensils. You will need a grate, a trivet to support pots, and cookware made of cast iron. The most useful for starting out are a frying pan with a lid and a large Dutch oven. (If you have the pans but no lids, use double or triple layers of aluminum foil tightly sealed at the rim.) You might want to acquire one extra item: a tin reflecting oven is good for baking or roasting in front of the fire and can be either homemade or found through camping suppliers. With this preparation, you'll be able to cook great food, even during long power outages.

First, build a good fire using hardwood, then let it burn down until there is a bed of hot coals, which will produce long-lasting heat. Do not use softwood because it does not leave hot coals. You are then ready to cook on a trivet, bake in the ashes, roast meat on a dangle spit, or use a reflecting oven. Your previous experience and common sense will help you calculate the correct timing for each item of food.

Trivet

Place the trivet on the side of the fire, heap hot coals underneath, and put the pot of water, soup, or stew on top. The hot coals will bring the liquid to a boil and then, as the heat lessens, it will simmer quietly.

The Dutch Oven

This pot can be used on a trivet or nestled in the coals. You can cook pies, soda breads, and casseroles in oven-safe dishes; to keep the bottom from burning, place a small trivet inside the oven. Heap coals on the lid and check at regular intervals. If the food is cooking too quickly, remove coals from the lid; if too slowly, add more coals.

Ashes

Potatoes and vegetables with thick skins, like acorn squash, can be buried in gray ashes and then topped with hot coals. This also works for fish and other vegetables in foil packages. In earlier times, these would have been placed in a natural wrapper such as soaked green corn husks.

Spit

To make a simple spit, tie meat securely with butcher's twine and attach the other end to the mantelpiece or damper handle. The meat should be about three inches above the hearth and eight to ten inches from the fire. The heat and weight will cause the meat to rotate slowly, and the cook can help by twisting the twine now and then. A drip pan should be positioned directly underneath to catch the juices. The addition of a reflector on the hearthside will help cook the meat evenly. You can make one by covering a cookie sheet with foil and propping it up in front of the roast with bricks, a concrete block, cooking pot, or other fireproof item.

Reflecting Oven

Usually made of tin, these three-sided ovens sit on the hearth and reflect the heat from the fire back towards the meat or pot. They have hooks or spits from which small birds or pieces of meat can be hung. Alternately, they can serve as baking ovens when pots are placed inside and rotated during cooking for even heat.

Spit

To make a simple spit, tie meat securely with butcher's twine and attach the other end to the mantelpiece or damper handle. The meat should be about three inches above the hearth and eight to ten inches from the fire. The heat and weight will cause the meat to rotate slowly, and the cook can help by twisting the twine now and then. A drip pan should be positioned directly underneath to catch the juices. The addition of a reflector on the hearthside will help cook the meat evenly. You can make one by covering a cookie sheet with foil and propping it up in front of the roast with bricks, a concrete block, cooking pot, or other fireproof item.

Stoves

When I was working on a project with the Frank Lloyd Wright Foundation, I was lucky enough to meet people who, as young admirers of his work, had him design their houses. He would listen to their needs, and then build for them what he thought they should have. True to his Welsh-Celtic heritage, no matter how modern the homes, he gave them impressive, and usually very wide, fireplaces of stone, brick, or concrete. Sometimes these fireplaces had true inglenooks, sometimes hearths that were reflecting pools to catch the patterns made by the elements of fire and water. For one couple, Wright designed andirons to stand more than a yard apart. Over the years, the couple grew tired of lugging four-foot logs into the living room. So, unknown to Mr. Wright, they fitted a neat matte-black stove into the space, hoping it would escape his attention on his periodic visits.

For fireplace lovers, woodstoves will never quite do. I like both and know that one day we will have a stove. We will still be able to enjoy the flames and will have much less fine dust around the house. In Scandinavia and Russia, magnificent tiled stoves—though no flames show—are still the center of attention.

The woodstove today is a clever and friendly piece of engineering available in many sizes and colors. If you spend time looking, you can find one—either new or old —that is just right for your own situation. In general, a stove that is too small might not produce enough heat, while one that is too large can cause overheating. You can get information from local dealers or other professionals about the correct size for the number of cubic feet in your room as well as the winter temperatures and wind conditions in your area, plus installation facts. A friend of ours found a suitable and practically new Vermont Castings stove at a great price through her local newspaper, simply because the new owner of a house didn't want a stove.

New woodstoves are designed to get the most heat possible out of the wood they burn. They are airtight, airflow can be adjusted to the exact rate needed, and they can be left alone for many hours—even overnight—to generate steady warmth. Today's stoves also have built-in baffles, or chambers, that absorb the heat and radiate it into the room. Some are even sophisticated enough to have a thermostat that opens and closes the draft regulator, controlling the rate at which the fire burns.

Of course, you may come across an old stove with great character. But before you buy it, check for cracks and missing parts. Cracks in the firebox are a big problem. Sometimes—but not always—they can be repaired by a specialist. Cracks in other parts that are not subject to such intense heat can be mended with stove putty. There are places around the country where you can order parts for old stoves. Make sure you can find the piece you need before you buy your stove. A woodstove with rust on the outside can be taken care of with elbow grease and a wire brush followed by polishing with stove black. Rust on the inside is another matter. Important working parts that are rusted through may be expensive or even impossible to fix.

Once the woodstove has been correctly installed, and you learn how to operate the draft regulator and chimney damper in relation to the temperature and wind, your stove should give off steady heat. During the learning period, any smoking will probably be due to incorrect air regulation, or, as mentioned, you may need to crack a window if the house is too airtight.

There are many sad tales of wonderful country houses burned to the ground because ashes were removed from a stove or fireplace, emptied into a paper bag or other flammable container, and then set on the porch. Be sure to put ashes into a metal container with a cover and let them sit outside on the ground until they are completely dead. Only then should ashes be transferred to a bag or trash can to save for use in the garden. Also, remember to keep combustibles like curtains, clothes, or furniture a minimum of three feet away from the woodstove, and have a fire extinguisher handy.

Just as in fireplaces, burning wood in stoves causes creosote build-up in the chimney. If it is not removed regularly, sparks can start a fire. With occasional use, the chimney will probably need to be cleaned once a year. However, if you burn the stove every day, the chimney may require cleaning as often as every six months. Frequent creosote build-up may indicate the stove is operating at too slow a burn rate. For details on how to deal with a chimney fire, see page 85.

Firewood

After you have made sure that all chimneys, fireplaces, or woodstoves are in proper working condition, it is time to build a woodpile of seasoned hardwood. "Seasoned" wood has been dried from four to twelve months, "hardwood" refers to heavy wood that provides a long burn and gives out steady heat. It will not cause as fast a creosote buildup and will generally smoke and spark less than softwood. The hardwoods with the highest BTU ratings are shagbark hickory, black locust, white ash, red and white oak, beech, yellow birch, sugar maple, and cherry. Adding a few pieces of fragrant wood, like apple and cherry, is a luxury and especially delightful.

You can obtain this fuel by contacting local suppliers or by cutting fallen and dying trees on your own property. Once you know your area, you can scout other sources for wood to buy cheaply or get free: state or national parks, local orchards, town landfills, or private owners who want their land cleaned up.

Wood is usually sold by the cord or by the "face" cord. Most people buy a face cord, a stack measuring four feet by eight feet with logs, or split wood, measuring one-to-two feet long. Wood is also sold by the truckload, with a standard half-ton pickup holding roughly one-third cord of wood. If you buy from your supplier in the spring you will get the best price and have dry, seasoned wood for use in the late fall and winter. However, if you wait until

the fall the price will rise. It's economical to stack the wood yourself — and great exercise. Just make sure the wood is left close to your shed or stacking site. The first time you use a supplier, be present for the delivery to see that you receive the correct amount and that the wood is indeed seasoned (look at the cut ends; dry wood will have cracks). If you specified mixed hardwoods, don't accept any pine, cedar, or other softwood. Newly cut wood or green wood is always cheaper, but you will have to plan ahead. Delivered in the spring, it should be ready for use during the second winter.

If you live in the Snowbelt, site the woodpile near your house so that it is easy to reach in the middle of winter. However, never place it directly against the house or inside, especially in the convenient cellar, because bugs from the logs will invade wood siding or supporting beams. Much well-seasoned wood is likely to have been dead when it was cut, and is often home to the bugs that killed it. Make a platform for the pile to rest on from bricks, or wood pallets, and then stack the wood. The stack can be stabilized by placing at least one end against a tree or fence. If you buy green wood, stack it in a crisscross pattern to allow air to circulate, and place it where there is sun for at least part of the day. In the fall, cover with a tarp to protect from snow, ice, and rain. Flat-bottomed children's sleds are an easy way to pull wood to the house across snow and mud.

Around the House

Most of us think of country houses as being white—and many prefer them so. The Shakers painted only their most important buildings white, the ultimate in neatness and purity. White paint was very expensive—not the whitewash of dairies and kitchen, but oil paint, which contained the most lead. Late in the 19th century, white was considered ordinary and a nuisance. Here's a report from the turn of the century.

Every few years certain colors are "in fashion," as are coats, hats or gloves. Thus various shades of gray were popular twenty-five years ago; then came the browns a few years later; then buffs and yellows with white or dark green trimmings; and at the present time shades of green are much used. In the thickly-settled village almost any of the above shades if not too bright and glaring, smoothly put on, are in harmony with the surroundings, but in the country soft colors of gray, brown, or buff are more appropriate. White, the typical color of New England country dwellings, and some other sections, is too glaring unless heavily set with trees and shrubbery. While white lead is perhaps the most durable of paints, it is easily soiled by contact with trees, or by water running down from the eaves, and often it costs more to keep a house looking nicely in white than in some other color.

From *The Small Country Place* by Samuel T. Maynard

Before ready-mixed paints became available, country people made their own or, if they could afford it, paid for the services of a colorman, or house painter. Here was an artisan who made his own materials and tools. He compounded marvelous but deadly mixtures of oil, drying agents, and pigments. The warm colors: soft yellows, some reds, and nearly all browns, came from earth and clay. Black came from the fine soot of oil lamps and burnt bone meal. Some colors were derived from plants and fruits, but the harsh, bright greens, blues, and purples had arsenic, lead, sulfur, and acids as necessary ingredients. Until portable mills were invented in the mid-19th century, making paint was hard work because the pigment and linseed oil had to be ground and mixed by hand. There were no flat-sided brushes at the time. There was one style of brush—and a steady hand.

Oil and pigment being mixed.

A portable paint mill.

A 19th-century brush at work.

These pictures were taken at Eastfield Village, about seven miles from my house. If you ever want to experience historic working methods of country blacksmiths, potters, paperhangers, timber framers, all manner of craftsmen, and true restoration, you can attend the workshops organized by Don Carpentier, the owner and creator of the village.

Country Walls

Tapestries were the first wall coverings, in addition to paintings hung here and there on wood-covered panels. Plain walls were becoming a bore for town dwellers at the end of the 18th century. Homeowners began to cover their walls with paper from China, England, and France that imitated the texture of silk and embossed leather patterns favored by the gentry. The designs copied subjects of popular paintings—flowers, vines, leaves, fruit, vases, and columns. Plain, clean walls survived longer in rural America, where wallpaper was considered too expensive. When a bit of fun and color was wanted, country people imitated wallpaper with hand-cut stencils—and made wonderful art at the same time. By the mid-19th century, American manufacturing took over. Today, most wallpaper is—and looks—cheaper than good paint. Many of the traditional designs have evolved into small patterns that originated in cloth made in colonial India. It was called chintz and has a "cottage" look that the British still love.

Just after World War II, there was a paper shortage in Europe. I can remember my grandfather, who was a skilled restorer of fine woodwork and cabinetry, making cardboard combs with different size teeth. He dipped them in wall paint and made intricate repetitive designs on the walls in his house. Sometimes, on a plain, wet, painted surface, he would "paint" with one of his combs, and with clever wristwork simulate wood grains—knots and all.

Right
I like the boldness of the stairway walls in the historic Peter Wentz house in Pennsylvania. The person using the paint sponge avoided regimentation to produce this lively effect.

Kerosene Lamps

With the introduction of kerosene, lamps replaced candles and made it possible for people to sew or read in the evening. Indeed, many houses in the country used kerosene lamps well into the 20th century, when the Rural Electrification Administration finally brought them power. Long-burning and relatively safe, these lamps still provide good light when acts of nature, such as ice and snowstorms, high winds, and tornadoes, knock out your electricity for days. Even when repair crews are working around the clock, main lines are fixed first and individual lines last (as I have learned from experience). Keep a couple of kerosene lamps on hand to give rooms a cheery glow and enough light to cook, play games, and read. They are readily available at most country hardware stores, along with cans for kerosene storage.

An old household hint recommends soaking a new wick in vinegar and then drying it before insertion to make the lamp burn better and smoke less. Also, pinch or cut off the burned portion of the wick when the lamp is cool, and wash the chimney before the next use. For safety, do not place the lamp where it can be turned over easily, too close to the ceiling, or near flammable fabric.

A lamp that is nightly in use should be trimmed and replenished regularly every morning, otherwise there will be no certainty in its burning, and it will go out unexpectedly at any time in the evening, leaving the room in darkness. After you have removed the shade and glass chimney, raise the wick by turning the screw towards the right hand, and cut off with the lamp-scissors, or nip off with your thumb and finger the edge of the wick that has been burning the night before; but do not trim it too closely, or you will find it difficult to light again. It is sufficient, barely to cut off the rim of the brown crust. When you find that the wick is reduced by burning, to only about an inch and a half in length, it is time to take it out and put in a new one. In winter, a new wick will be required once a week; in the short summer evenings, it will of course last longer. Always do the wick before the oil. Clean out every morning, the cup or candlestick part that catches the droppings. Wipe out with a clean soft cloth... the glass chimney, and the shade; and dust well their outsides, and also every part of the lamp. Then replace it on the table to be ready for evening.

From *Miss Leslie's House Book*, 1840

Caring for Furniture

Old furniture acquires a beautiful patina over time. It is a look acquired after years of exposure to sunlight, air, polishing, and use. The wood becomes colored with a subtlety unmatched by stain from a can. There are still pieces of furniture, to be found in antiques stores or at auctions, whose original patina can be preserved. This is especially true of mahogany, walnut, maple, or cherry with an old finish. It's important to decide if a piece of furniture can be restored, because stripping will remove in minutes what took years to create.

If your piece of furniture looks as if the original finish might be retained, the first step is to clean it thoroughly to get rid of the years of accumulated dirt and grease. Start by dipping a cotton cloth in a solution of equal parts mineral oil, turpentine, and white vinegar to remove dirt and old wax. Squeeze the excess from the cloth, and rub with the grain. Test a small, concealed area in order to see what effect this has on the finish. Then you will know how to proceed with the rest of the surface. Wipe a small section at a time, and dry with a clean cotton cloth before going on to the next section. Give the whole piece another wipe with a fresh cloth, and let it dry for at least twenty-four hours. Next, apply one or two thin coats of good quality paste wax, buffing well after each coat.

Often you will find furniture with old shellac or varnish that is sticky. In this case, use #0000 steel wool, which is very fine. Dip a steel wool pad in mineral spirits and rub lightly along the grain of the wood, removing only the build-up of dirt and wax, not the finish. Follow by wiping with a soft cotton cloth. If there is good coverage left, polish with paste wax, and buff. However, if the old finish disappears, you might want to refinish.

You may find a chest that has been stored in a humid place, and the drawers might smell musty. To remedy this, remove any paper linings, vacuum thoroughly, then air the drawers for several days, preferably in sunlight. Next, place a saucer of baking soda in each drawer, replace the drawers in the chest, and let stand for a week, refreshing the baking soda if necessary. If this does not solve the problem, you can sand the insides of the drawers and paint on a coat of sealer to lock in the smell.

White spots or rings on a table or chest are caused by water and indicate the water did not go all the way through the finish. You might be able to remove the marks by sprinkling table salt on the spot and then rubbing gently—always with the grain—with a cloth dampened with mineral oil. The abrasion will dull the finish a bit, but you can bring back the shine with paste wax.

Cracks in wood surfaces, produced by use and dry conditions, can be filled with wood putty. Powdered putty is the recommended type because it will absorb a stain to match the old wood. Follow the mixing instructions, force it into the cracks, and smooth out. When it is hard and dry, sand and stain.

In rural areas, furniture was usually constructed by farmers and settlers themselves to serve a need and to fit a specific place. For example, corner cupboards were built to fit, then painted not only to protect the wood but also to add color to a plain room. At first, country furniture was painted reddish brown, brown, or black, followed later by blue, green, gray, or ochre. These colors came from berries, organic matter, or clays mixed with water, milk, or linseed oil. For example, reds were created from berries or powdered iron oxide, which could produce shades of red-brown, light red, and maroon; black could be obtained by mixing chimney soot with linseed oil. During the 18th century, painted furniture was embellished with various patterns created by the use of feathers, combs, and sponges. At the same time, these techniques, along with stencils, were used on walls in the house.

If you find a piece of furniture that you think is truly old, remember that it should have a faded look after years of exposure to sun and dirt, and it should also show signs of wear. Look carefully, because wear can be faked with steel wool. Old paint, if scraped, comes as powder, but new paint will come off in pieces or ribbons. Also, check the underside of the piece as well as the back, and be suspicious—especially if there is paint where a frugal country person would not waste it.

Saw marks help tell the story of a piece of furniture, especially its age. Early marks were straight, made by saws driven by windmills and waterwheels. Then, around 1850, the circular saw powered by steam engines came into use. This type of saw left curved marks. Nails and screws also help determine the age of furniture. Hand-forged nails were pointed and had round or rectangular heads. By 1815, machinery came along that made nails with square heads and blunt ends. These were used until the end of the 1800s, when round-headed nails with pointed ends came on the scene. The first screws were made of hand-cut wood; they were replaced by machine-made screws at the beginning of the 1800s. These screws had even threads and blunt ends. Pointed ends came into use in the second half of the 1800s.

This Windsor chair was given to us by a friend. Her husband, who used it every day for more than forty years, gradually wore off the original finish and polished the bare wood on the arms to give them a lovely golden glow.

Many chairs were made with cane, rush, or splint seats, which eventually sag from use. To tighten, soak the underside of the seat with water and hang it upside down. As the natural material dries, it should tighten and make the chair usable again.

In most cases, wood furniture originally was painted for a purpose, often to disguise a mixture of secondary woods or unappealing woods or common pine. This is true for furniture ranging from Windsor chairs of the 1700s to Hoosier kitchen cabinets in the 1800s. For example, some chairs and Hoosier cabinets were made from four or five different kinds of wood, then painted. What makes these painted pieces appealing is not the wood but the finish that often has acquired a lovely patina over the years. They can be cleaned in sections by wiping lightly with an equal solution of turpentine and mineral oil (years ago called paraffin oil), and then drying with clean cloths. The surface can then be sealed by waxing. If a piece is too battered to clean, it is better to repaint than to refinish.

Chair Repair

There is a great deal of stress where the seat of a chair joins the back. If this joint becomes loose, the two pieces move when the chair is used, and other joints start to loosen. A rung is usually first to be affected by the motion and will work its way out of the leg.

The old glue on the end of the rung and inside the fitting can be softened by pouring hot vinegar on it. Any glue that does not dissolve after a few minutes can be gently scraped off, and the area can then be dried.

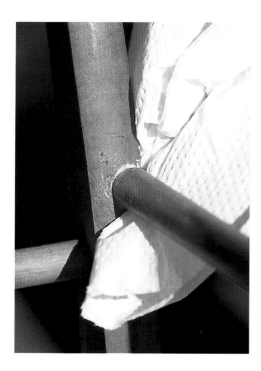

Next, carpenter's wood glue should be applied and the rung placed back in its hole. Carefully remove all excess glue.

Hold the two pieces firmly together while the glue dries; tie with rope or use a bungee cord. Wait twenty-four hours before using.

This is a view of the lean-to kitchen at the 1660 Thomas Lee House in coastal Connecticut, showing a ship's knee brace supporting the beam. The room is remarkably unchanged. The Shakers, who invented the flat broom, always hung them like this. It does not take long for a broom that stands on the floor to lose its shape, the spring in its bristles, and its effectiveness. In a different environment, the oak floor could be preserved and have the cracks filled in the following way:

Soak some newspaper in water, mash it into pulp, squeeze it out, and put it in a bucket. Then mix powdered glue with water in a separate container until it is smooth and flowing. Add the glue to the pulp, stirring well, and blend into the mixture a dry earth color that matches the filler to the floorboard. Place in the cracks, remove the excess, and let the floor dry thoroughly before sanding.

Country Household Hints

Gathered from books published in the 19th century, such as Mrs. Child's *The American Frugal Housewife*, are selected items of household advice that show how things were kept clean and sparkling. They are presented here, in large part, as they were written. Indeed, many of these natural cleaners are still effective.

Baskets

Appy equal parts of boiled linseed oil and turpentine to baskets to clean and prevent drying. Then wipe off excess with a dry cloth.

To clean, first scrub with lye from the wash tub, and then rinse with strong salt water.

Brass

Crushed coarse rhubarb leaves will clean both brass and copper.

Mix equal parts of salt and flour and moisten with vinegar to make a thick paste. Apply with a damp cloth. Then wash and dry.

Shine unvarnished beds with half a lemon dipped in salt. After washing and drying, rub the brass with rottenstone (Note: this is a finely ground natural limestone powder).

Rottenstone and oil are proper materials for cleaning brasses. If wiped every morning with flannel and New England rum, they will not need to be cleaned half as often.

Brooms

To make a new broom last longer, soak in hot salt water before using.

Carpets

Cut the heart of a cabbage in half. Using it like a brush, go over the carpet to clean.

Coat grease spots with a layer of cornmeal, rub into the carpet and let stand overnight. Then brush up cornmeal.

To sweep carpets clean, first sprinkle with fresh grass clippings or with fresh, dry powder snow.

Clean a dirty carpet by scattering grated raw potatoes and then brushing vigorously.

Copper

To remove tarnish, clean it with half a lemon dipped in a mixture of one tablespon of salt and one tablespoon of vinegar.

Crush a raw onion with damp earth and use as a polish.

Dampen an old cloth and rub fine sand on the pieces until they gleam. Procure very fine sand from ant hills.

Dampness

To reduce dampness in closets, wrap twelve pices of chalk together and hang them up.

Fireplace

When the fire is burning brightly, toss in a handful of salt to act as a cleaner.

To remove soot and grit from inside the chimney, place a couple handfuls of common bay salt hay on the fire.

Floors

Clean varnished floors and woodwork with cold tea to bring out their shine.

Before sweeping a dusty floor, sprinkle with damp tea leaves, or fresh grass cuttings. They will collect the dust, and prevent it from rising onto the bedding and furniture.

Furniture

To remove minor white marks from wooden furniture, rub with a paste made of olive oil mixed with cigar ashes. Then polish off with a soft cloth.

To blend in small surface scratches, rub with the broken edge of a piece of walnut meat and polish with a soft cloth.

Give a fine soft polish to varnished furniture by rubbing with pulverized rottenstone and linseed oil, and afterwards wipe clean with a soft silk rag.

Glass

Clean a glass bottle or decanter by filling with soapy water and adding a couple tablespoons of vinegar.

Wipe crystals from chandelier with two parts vinegar to three parts water, then rinse and dry.

Gold

Polish gold by using a soft cloth and a paste made of cigar ashes and water.

Ice

Put hay on icy steps in the winter to prevent slipping. Keep a bale beside the door you ordinarily use. It won't track into the house like ashes or salt.

Knives

Clean and polish the blades with fireplace ashes.

Leather

Clean leather by rubbing with equal parts of vinegar and boiled linseed oil, and then polish with a cloth.

Beat the whites of three eggs and rub them with a soft cloth into a leather chair. The leather will soon be clean and shine as if new.

Odor

Simmer vinegar on the stove to get rid of unpleasant cooking odors.

Put out a cut onion and leave until it has drawn unpleasant smells to itself and then throw it away.

Paint

Hardened paint on brushes can be softened by soaking in boiling vinegar. Afterwards wash in hot soapy water.

Remove paint from glass by applying hot vinegar with a cloth. After it is softened, scrape off gently.

Pests

To keep ants away from the house, sprinkle dried and powdered leaves of tansy and pennyroyal on doorsteps and window ledges.

Freshly cut pennyroyal placed in a room, or drops of oil sprinkled about, will keep away mosquitoes.

Tansy or pennyroyal will keep away fleas. Rub cats and dogs with fresh-cut pennyroyal once a week.

When bedbugs lodge in the wall, fill any apertures with a mixture of soft soap and snuff. Take the bedstead apart and treat in the same way.

Make flypaper by spreading on paper a mixture of melted resin and enough lard or oil to make it, when cold, the consistency of honey.

A muslin bag filled with pounded cloves and placed on the pantry shelf will keep flour and grains free of weevils.

To keep moths away, procure shavings of cedar wood, enclose in muslin bags, and place in chests, drawers, and closets with woolen clothing.

Pewter

When polish is gone off, first rub on the outside with a little sweet oil (olive oil) on a piece of soft linen; then clear oil off with pure whiting (powdered chalk) on linen cloths.

Silver

Soak tarnished silverware in sour milk for half an hour. Then wash in soapy water and dry.

Soak tarnished silver in potato water for several hours.

For scratches use a paste of olive oil and whiting and rub with a soft cloth.

Make a paste of baking soda and water and scrub with a soft brush.

Stains

Moisten fruit stains with glycerine, let stand for several minutes and rinse.

Hold fabric with stains from berries and juices over a basin and pour boiling water through. Then wash with soap and rinse.

Dip clothing with fresh bloodstains in salted water, to remove or diminish stain.

Tea-stained cloth should be rubbed with a mixture of one tablespoon of salt and one cup of soft soap and then placed outside in the sun for a day, before laundering.

Wallpaper

Make a smooth paste of equal parts of cornstarch and water and rub on wallpaper spots. When it is dry, brush off and spots will be gone.

Wax

Place a blotter on candle wax, and then hold a hot iron over the blotter which will absorb the melted wax.

Windows

To clean, rub down with kerosene on newspapers. Especially good for rain spots.

Wash with a mixture of one part vinegar to ten parts warm water.

The always busy, clean, and efficient kitchen at Hancock Shaker Village.

Country Remedies

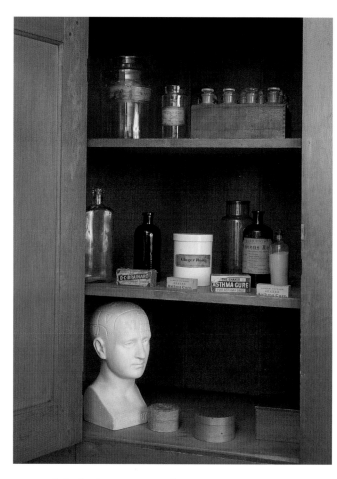

A good deal of country wisdom concerns how to look after various aches, pains, and ailments. Since doctors were few and far between, families had to care for themselves. They looked to the advice that was handed down through the generations from their own immigrant group, and from the Native Americans in their area. Included here—mostly as written—are some examples of American folk medicine and folklore commonly found in old sources. Some are delightful and probably worked due to the placebo effect, while others—those using herbs or fruits—may actually have beneficial effects. Then there are some remedies that simply sound outrageous. You might recall hearing one or two of the following cures mentioned in your own family. I should also add that these remedies are to be relished for their interest, rather than heeded.

Abscess or Boil

Tie bread in a white cloth, dip it in boiling water and place on the abscess overnight.

Press a cabbage leaf dipped in hot water on the abscess.

Cover the area with a slice of onion, and wrap with a clean cloth.

Apply a poultice made of crushed burdock leaves, or one made of ginger and flour, to draw boil to a head.

Bruises

Treat a bruise by applying brown paper coated with molasses.

Ease the pain by rubbing with an onion.

Bathe with an infusion of hyssop leaves.

Burns

Honey applied to burns will help the pain and prevent blisters from forming.

Soak a soft cloth in cod-liver oil and place it on the burn.

Mix corn meal with powdered charcoal and add milk to make a paste for the burn.

Tie a piece of suet over the burn for quick healing.

Apply apple cider vinegar to affected area to remove soreness.

The pain of sunburn is eased by bathing frequently with cider vinegar.

Colds

When a cold is coming on, put blackberry cordial in a mug and top up with hot water. Drink the cordial in bed and go to sleep.

Drink hot milk with crushed garlic in it.

Spread goose grease on brown paper and put it on your chest.

Eat a hot roasted onion before going to bed to cure a cold.

Catnip and pennyroyal teas are both good for a cold.

Soak feet in hot water to get rid of a cold.

To clear head congestion, boil vinegar and water in a pot. Remove it from the heat and place your head, covered with a cloth, over the pot and inhale.

Drink whiskey heated with sugar and lemon, before going to bed.

Feed a cold and starve a fever.

Put your hat on the bedpost, get in bed and drink whiskey until you see two hats.

Corns

Bind on bread soaked in vinegar to remove corns. Reapply mornings and evenings.

Burn willow bark, and then mix the ashes with vinegar and apply to the corn.

Insert the toe in a lemon. Keep it on during the night. The corn can then be easily removed.

Corns should be treated with roasted onions mashed together and used as a poultice.

Soak feet in hot soapy water with vinegar to soften the corn.

Bind ivy leaves and vinegar onto the corn with a cloth.

Rub every day with a cut clove of garlic.

Cut corns in the waning moon and they will gradually disappear.

In 1902, Sears, Roebuck sold this 55¢ cure for corns and bunions. Early commercially made shoes sold to rural people were often limited in sizes and fit. The ball end of this tool was placed inside the shoe, leaving the ring outside. The handles were gently closed, stretching the leather over the painful spot without distorting the rest of the shoe.

Coughs

Slice an onion very thin, and alternate layers of onion and sugar. Place a plate on top to weigh them down. The juice that forms is soothing for a cough and safe for children.

Chop two large turnip roots into small pieces, and boil in a quart of water. Cool and strain. Add an amount of honey equal to whatever portion is taken.

Take a spoonful of kerosene mixed with sugar.

Cramps

Cramps in the neck or legs can be relieved by an application of whiskey and red pepper.

Drink warm pennyroyal tea.

Tie periwinkle stems around the leg or arm that is likely to be affected.

Cuts and Wounds

Remove the inside skin, or coating, from the shell of an uncooked egg. Place its moist side on a cut to promote healing.

Bathe the cut in a solution of water and baking soda. Sprinkle it, while still wet, with black pepper.

Cover a large cut with cow dung which is soft and creates heat. The cut will heal quickly.

Apply cobwebs to stop cuts from bleeding.

Press yarrow leaves to a cut to stop the flow of blood.

Bathe cuts with an infusion of marigold leaves to ease pain and lessen scarring.

Sprinkle the dried, powdered leaves of wild sunflowers on the wound to arrest blood flow.

Use a moist wad of chewing tobacco as a poultice.

Bruise peach tree leaves and put on the wound. Repeat as needed.

Diarrhea

In the summer, eat fresh blackberries, or boil blackberries in water, strain and drink the liquid.

Stew up garden rhubarb with some sugar, and eat a spoonful as long as necessary.

A tablespoonful of W.I. rum, a tablespoonful of molasses, and the same quantity of olive oil, well simmered together is helpful for this disorder.

Flour boiled thoroughly in milk, so as to make quite a thick porridge is good.

Flannel wet with brandy, powdered with cayenne pepper, and laid upon the bowels affords great relief in extreme distress.

Earache

To alleviate the slight earache, blow pipe or cigarette smoke into the ear.

To cure an earache, insert a piece of hot onion into the ear.

Put a few drops of hot sweet oil (olive oil) into the ear and plug with cotton.

Eyes

Black eyes can be eased by using a grated apple poultice.

Sore eyes can be treated with an eye wash made of apple juice.

Soak bread in a little milk and tie over the eye, and leave over night to relieve inflammation.

To help soreness, apply fresh green plantain leaves to the eyelids.

Cure a sty by putting grated potatoes, covered by a cloth, on the eye.

Wash weeping eyes with chamomile tea at night and in the morning

Feet

For offensive odor, soak feet in water in which green bark of oak has been boiled.

For excessive perspiration, put bran or oatmeal into the socks.

To relieve itching feet, soak every day in cider vinegar.

Fever
Pound horseradish leaves into a pulp. Apply to the soles of the feet to draw out fever.

Break a fever by drinking hot ginger tea.

Put slices of raw potato on the forehead to draw out a fever.

Hair
To make hair thicker, massage the juice of watercress into the scalp.

To get rid of dandruff, massage vinegar into scalp several times a week.

Hay Fever
Steep rose petals in a cup of hot water. Strain and apply drops to the eyes during the day to relieve irritation.

Mix leaves and flowers of goldenrod and ragweed. Put one-half ounce of the herbs in two cups of boiling water and allow to steep for ten minutes. Drink a small glassful four times a day to cure hay fever.

Headaches
Drink chamomile tea to soothe the head.

Bathe the forehead with hot water in which mint or sage has been boiled.

Cure a headache by swallowing a spider web.

Soak a cloth in warm vinegar and apply to the forehead.

Poison ivy or oak.
Mix powdered lime with lard until you have a paste and spread on the rash.

Apply milk, heavily salted, to skin affected by poison ivy. Allow to dry.

Slit the stem of jewelweed, and rub its sticky juice directly on the skin and let dry. When it starts to itch, reapply.

Squeeze the milk from the stems of milkweed and apply it to the rash.

Juice squeezed from the leaf of the elderberry and applied directly to the inflamed area will relieve the itch. Continue until the rash is gone.

Rheumatism and Arthritis
Keep rheumatism away by carrying a potato in the pocket, unseen by the opposite sex. The smaller and harder it becomes, the less likely the suffering from rheumatism.

Rub the aching limb with oil of mustard.

Take a teaspoon of cider vinegar every morning before breakfast.

Drink an infusion of marigold flowers four times a day.

Mix two teaspoons of cider vinegar and two teaspoons of honey into one-half cup warm water and drink three times a day.

Sore Throat
Gargle with warm, salt water.

Drink hot sage tea

Gargle with warm tea made from slippery elm bark.

Sugar and brandy relieves a sore throat.

A stocking bound on warm from the foot, at night, is good for the sore throat.

Stings and bites
Rub the spot with mashed plantain leaves.

Dab bee stings with household ammonia.

Rub dock leaf on insect stings, and also on nettle stings.

Apply mud to insect bites to relieve pain.

Dab stings with vinegar.

A slice of onion applied to an insect sting will take the pain away.

Rub vinegar or lemon juice on insect bites to eliminate the itch.

Stomach
Eat fresh mint or drink mint tea to settle an upset stomach.

Drink chamomile tea for an upset stomach.

Place crushed horseradish leaves directly on the skin over the stomach for aching.

Chop a clove of garlic and cover with a cup of boiling water. Drink when cool for indigestion.

Tea made from sheep droppings is good for stomach troubles.

Stop morning sickness by drinking a glass of water with a teaspoonful of vinegar upon rising.

A spoonful of ashes stirred in cider is good to prevent sickness at the stomach.

Teeth
To relieve a toothache, chew the leaves of catnip.

Treat toothache by putting a clove in the tooth, or using clove oil.

Whiten teeth by rubbing with powdered charcoal.

Prevent toothache by carrying a rabbit's tooth.

Warts
To remove warts, rub them with green walnuts.

Apply crushed marigold leaves and their juices to warts.

If horsehair is wrapped tightly around a wart, it will drop off.

Rub a snail on a wart to make it disappear.

Rub the wart with the furry inside of a broad bean pod.

The Weather

Weather Wisdom

When I was a child, I used to cross from one side of an estuary in Essex to a small island called Mersea. Our ferryman and his boat worked the oyster beds in the odd hours. Reuben was small and tough, with a weathered old face. He wore aged canvas pants, an old blue jersey, and boots that were folded above his knees. He did not have many teeth, and was the first man I'd ever seen with an earring. As we cast off with six passengers, it was clear, windy, and cold—typical for late May. Someone who had to return later asked about getting a trip back, because of the tide changes. Reuben looked up at the sky and said, "No later than three," because bad weather was on its way. We all looked at the white clouds scurrying along up in the blue and tried to guess what he meant. "I heard it on the weather forecast," he said.

For thousands of years, humans have devoted time and energy to the science of weather. Long before our sophisticated computer era, we watched the movements of the planets and the earth, we noted the directions of the winds and their effects, and we studied the actions and reactions of animals, insects, and plants. Today we recognize that the old ways—many with a saying or rhyme to carry the information—are sometimes as reliable as our modern methods.

For example, birds, animals, and insects are especially sensitive to changes in air pressure, and will alter their behavior before a storm. Cows tend to stay huddled together near the pasture gate if the weather is threatening, but they stroll around the pasture if it is going to be fine. They lie on the ground when it is going to rain, supposedly to keep themselves a dry spot on the grass. Frogs have a tendency to increase their serenading several hours before an incoming storm because the increased humidity keeps their skin moist and allows them to stay out of the water longer. And bees stick close to the hive before a storm.

Tornadoes

Tornadoes are extremely violent storms with intense winds in their vortex, which occur where cold and warm fronts collide. Updrafts in the center of the typical funnel cloud, which have been recorded at hundreds of miles per hour, can draw anything into the air and drop it some distance away. Once on the ground, tornadoes produce a terrifying roar. If your house is located in the central U.S., which has more tornadoes than anywhere else, or in any area known to have tornado activity, consult with your local authorities and prepare ahead of time. Watch thunder clouds for signs of a funnel, and have a plan of action for everyone in the family to follow. Many television and radio stations now have instant reporting systems that can track a tornado and give warning. Keep a portable radio with working batteries handy, as transmission wires are likely to be severed. If you have no "cyclone cellar," but do have a basement, position yourself in the southwest corner. Since tornadoes generally come from the southwest, if your house is hit, pieces are more likely to fall towards the northeast.

Lightning

We are all used to the thunder and lightning that occur throughout the country, generally on hot and humid afternoons and evenings. Lightning is a discharge of electricity that usually follows the easiest way to the ground. The high voltage can burn trees, damage buildings, cause combustible material to ignite, and kill people and animals. If you are indoors and see a storm approaching, unplug key electrical items such as computers and telephones, since lightning may enter the house through power or telephone lines. Stay away from open doors or windows. If you are outdoors, avoid any high place and get into a building. If there is no immediate shelter, look for a ditch or low spot to lie in or crouch down in the middle of a clump of trees. Do not get near or under a single tree since this is like being next to a lightning rod. Metal items, from backpacks to tractors, can also be dangerous in an electrical storm.

Altocumulus are mid-altitude clouds consisting of a layer of small cloudlets. They usually predict thunderstorms or rain within twenty-four hours.

Altostratus are mid-altitude clouds that block the light of the sun but are high enough to cast no shadows. Striated and dark gray in color, a darkening of this cloud cover indicates precipitation.

Cirrocumulus are high-altitude clouds that consist of a thin layer of ice crystals broken into bands or rows of small tufts by rising currents of air. They indicate unstable air and may lead to immediate precipitation.

Cirrocumulus undulatus are sheets of cirrocumulus with waves or undulations produced by the wind.

Cirrostratus are high-altitude clouds that consist of ice crystals and are spread out over a large area. Halos are sometime seen around these clouds, indicating precipitation.

Cirrus clouds are delicate, wispy swirls formed by high-altitude winds. They are often called mares' tails.

Cold fronts are the start of an air mass that is replacing warm air. It usually moves faster than a warm front and often brings brief, heavy rain.

Cumulonimbus are very large, thick clouds formed by strong thermals of moist, rising air that often reach a height of twelve miles where the jet stream shears off their tops and gives them the shape of anvils. Cumulonimbus clouds produce heavy rain and thunderstorms.

Cumulus, also called fair-weather cumulus, are small, white clouds with rounded tops and flattened bottoms. They form when the air is being warmed by the earth.

A typical anvil-shaped cumulonimbus cloud, which produces heavy rain and thunderstorms.

These cirrus clouds are commonly called mares' tails because their shape resembles the tail of a running horse. They sometimes precede a warm front that brings rain.

A lenticular cloud forms when moist air rises and condenses at the peak of a mountain. Since this condition only occurs at the peak, the cloud remains stationary.

Cumulus congestus clouds, darker on the bottom with peaks at the top, forming over the Florida Keys.

The sun hits drops of mist and is reflected back as a rainbow as this storm moves across Jackson Hole, Wyoming.

*"Red sky at night, shepherd's delight. Red sky in morning, shepherds take warning."
A red evening sky means the next day will be clear and calm, while red in the morning predicts rain before the day is out.*

A *dust devil* is a small, spinning column of rising dust and air that occurs when the sun heats the ground. When it hits cooler ground, it loses its energy and disappears.

Frontal fog develops in advance of a warm front, when rain falling through cold air ahead of the front forms a mist near the ground.

Ground fog forms when the cold ground chills the air just above it. This fog is often seen early in the morning, before it is evaporated by the sun.

Hurricanes are tropical cyclones that form over warm ocean water. The wind must reach a speed of at least seventy-five miles an hour to qualify as a hurricane.

Nimbostratus, the largest of the low-altitude clouds, are thick and gray. They accompany a low-pressure front and produce heavy rain or snow.

Stratocumulus are low-altitude clouds seen when a stratus cloud breaks apart or when cumulus clouds come together at the same altitude.

Stratus are low-altitude, gray clouds that usually form when the earth's surface cools. Stratus clouds may result in drizzle or light snow.

A *tornado* is a violent and rapidly spinning vortex of air that has been generated in a thunderstorm.

Tropical storms are formed over the ocean and often develop into hurricanes as the winds accelerate their speed.

A *warm front* is the edge of a slow-moving air mass that is warmer than the one it is replacing. It is usually accompanied by precipitation.

This dark, low nimbostratus cloud, which will produce rain, comes along with a low pressure front.

The front has now moved in over the same landscape, resulting in rain and gray skies.

Weather Lore

Whether the weather be cold,
Or whether the weather be hot,
We have to weather the weather
Whether we like it or not.

Red sky at night,
Shepherd's delight,
Red sky in the morning,
Shepherd's warning.

Dew in the night,
Next day will be bright

Grey mists at dawn,
The day will be warm

Rain before seven,
Fine before eleven.

A sun shiny shower,
Won't last half an hour

If the sun goes pale to bed,
'Twill rain tomorrow it is said.

Mackerel sky and mares' tails,
Make tall ships carry low sails.

Pale moon does rain,
Red moon does blow,
White moon does neither
rain nor snow.

When the stars begin to huddle,
The earth will soon become a puddle.

A rainbow at night,
Fair weather in sight.
A rainbow at morn,
Fair weather all gorn.

A foot deep of rain
Will kill hay and grain;
But three feet of snow,
Will make them grow mo'.

Who doffs his coat on a Winter's day,
Will gladly put it on in May.

Better to see a wolf in February
than a farmer in shirtsleeves

If February give much snow
A fine summer it doth foreshow.

Cows lying down in the pasture are harbingers of an approaching rainstorm.

Sheep leave higher elevations and head for low ground when weather threatens.

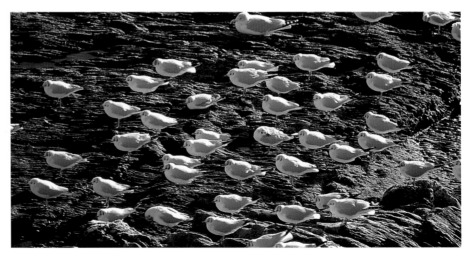

Gulls are often called "living weather vanes." They face into the wind so not to ruffle their feathers.

The rising sun colors these billowy cumulus, or fair-weather, clouds.

This tree attracted lightning that ran straight down the trunk to the ground. It's a clear example of why it makes sense to stay away from a tall tree during a thunderstorm.

If March comes in like a lion,
It goes out like a lamb.
If it comes in like a lamb,
It goes out like a lion.

A dry May and dripping June,
Brings everything in tune.

Dry August and warm
Doth harvest no harm.

Seagull, seagull,
get on the sand,
It's never fine weather
when you're on the land.

When a cow tries to scratch its ear,
It means a shower is very near.
When it clumps its side with its tail,
Look out for thunder, lightning and hail.

When the bees crowd out of their hive,
The weather makes it good to be alive.
When the bees crowd into their hive again,
It is a sign of thunder and rain.

Killing black beetles brings rain.

Onions skin very thin,
Mild winter coming in;
Onions skin thick and tough,
Coming winter will be rough.

Many holly berries, cold winter.

North wind brings hail,
South wind brings rain,
East winds we bewail,
West winds blow amain,
North-east wind is too cold,
South-east wind, not too warm,
North-west wind is far too bold,
South-west wind doth no harm

When the glass falls low,
Prepare for a blow;
When it rises high,
Let all your kites fly.

The weather's always ill
When the wind's not still

When the wind's in the East,
It's neither fit for man nor beast.

Those that are weatherwise
Are rarely otherwise.

A chopper made by Helen and Vernon Raaen in Tennessee. The steel blade was made from a disused industrial wood saw. The handle is made of dogwood that was being choked by a honeysuckle vine.

Art in the Country

Rural culture changes slowly, isolated as it is from urban centers. In the country, we are close to nature and the cycle of birth, death, and rebirth. Therefore, much of the art that country people like and make is strongly traditional. It is full of superstition, sentiment, and wisdom, celebrating planting, harvesting, and work. It is without pretension and full of sly humor—sometimes at the expense of city folk.

Northern Europe began to industrialize near the end of the 17th century, leaving rural pockets in the Celtic fringes of the British Isles, Brittany, Scandinavia, and elsewhere in poor political and economic condition but with their ways of making art intact. Many emigrants left for the New World, hoping for a better life and bringing their art with them. For example, though folk art in Britain is mostly a memory, it thrives among British descendants in modern-day Appalachia. Living on poor agricultural land and marooned in the hills as America developed around them, people could grow only enough for themselves. A barter system replaced nonexistent money, and talent and imagination came to the fore. Those who were handy with the whittling knife, axe, and saw used their abilities to carve, sculpt, and paint. They made their own tools and put their knowledge of plants to good use. When I was there, bushels of green tomatoes were exchanged for boxes of canning jars that were, in turn, used for honey from a basket-making friend's hives, and on and on. Homes are full of carvings, bowls, baskets, and pictures that were "put up" locally and acquired in transactions among families.

Visitors roaming the woods of southern Appalachia will not find much ginseng. Already scarce, this root, valued for its supposed powers to rejuvenate and to increase energy, has been picked over by people like Oscar Spenser, who has had to use his wits and knowledge of the wild to survive. As a young man, Spenser was seriously injured while at work four miles deep in a mine. As a result he lost a leg, for which he received no workers' compensation. Today he walks softly among the trees, looking for twisted woody-stemmed vines for walking sticks—and snakes, real or imagined. Some time ago, while he was looking for ginseng, a copperhead, much to its surprise, I'm sure, bit him on his artificial leg. That got him thinking about the way honeysuckle and other vines curl, snakelike, as they choke trees. He sold his first "snakes" as bird- and rodent-scarers to people with vegetable patches. Oscar now enjoys making them look more and more realistic, using fine tools to chisel every scale, bits of plastic insulation for tongues, and glass beads for eyes.

Minnie Adkins always looks relaxed and comfortable as she works, and most of her wooden menagerie is made on her lap in front of the television. All of her figures are full of fun, the way she is, as they emerge from a single basswood log. Minnie's pride in her work is exemplified when she relates that a collector told her that her carvings would have more value if she made them slightly different from each other. Her reply was that each figure was always as good as another, and that she tried to make them identical. Another collector, admiring her use of color, asked what mixture of pigments she used and was told that it was ready-mixed from Wal-Mart. This disarming quality is typical of people from Appalachia. She made me promise to let people know that the unpainted horse on the title page, was not properly finished.

In Connecticut, Carol Grant Hart weaves sculpture. This willow basket has no functional use but follows the supple form of a willow branch as it would curve in the wind. She says that the process of weaving infuses the basket itself with art, and may therefore take the viewer on a journey of imagination.

In West Virginia, Cher Shaffer makes all sorts of art: drawings, paintings, cutouts, bas reliefs, sculptures, scenes, and particularly, "haints—figures representing restless spirits returning from the grave. Her hands can do anything, and she creates instinctively. She is also a down-to-earth mother, homemaker, and rebel. She follows her instincts in a private corner of the basement family room that serves as her studio.

As a young girl in Georgia, she was much affected by the lives of black sharecropper families, who seemed to have more vivid lives than her own. Cut off by slavery from the visual art tradition of their African homeland, they amazed her with their spectacular spirituals and ghost stories.

Shapes and Symbols

The shapes of horse brasses, fraktur (illuminated lettering) papers, pie safes, quilts, painted chests, gravestones, and hex signs on barns all belong to rural life. Their origins are Celtic, Germanic, Scandinavian, Slavonic, Middle Eastern, and Asian. There is a sharing of symbols and proportion among these shapes. All of them have a simple and powerful integrity of pattern formed well before organized religions adopted some of the designs as their own. These folk art shapes show the limits of a world of creativity cut off from the culture of cities; they are simple, geometric, very symmetrical, illustrate the need for order in life, and reveal pride in workmanship.

No one quite knows from where, or when, these shapes originated. I don't think it matters. They are inspired doodles that are within us all, and were freely borrowed as people moved from one place to another. They are mostly circular images, often celestial, and speak not only of protection from the harm of the evil eye, disease, death, and disorder, but also of hope in the continuing rays of the sun and the rhythms of the moon. You will rarely see a cross, unlike elsewhere in the western world, except on Christian property.

The Cross, very rare—the early church frowned on the use of amulets with a cross motif

Three Hearts, said to give the horse long life

The Sun, Star, and Crescent, of Byzantine origin

The Swastika, the sign of Vishnu, the Hindu god of energy

Three Crescents, originated in Assyria, adopted by the Romans

The Wheel in Flame, a Buddhist symbol

The Crescent Moon, symbol of Isis, for protection against the evil eye

Solomon's Seal, considered to have powerful magical properties

When you see a massive Percheron or Clydesdale at a plowing contest or county fair, you will be looking at a descendant of a battle horse. In the Middle Ages, most plowing and pulling was done by oxen. Horses were bred to take the weight of the rider's arms and armor. The shining brasses of today have an even older history, dating back thousands of years to a time when mankind first began using horses to carry hunters and soldiers; bronze medallions were hung on harnesses as charms to protect horse and rider from harm.

The early use of amulets shaped like modern horse brasses was proven by the recent discovery of a chief's grave, over 2,000 years old, in Siberia. The bodies of seven mummified horses were preserved in perfect condition by the frost. The horses had complete bronze trappings, with designs almost identical to those seen today. In the 19th century, machinery that could stamp out many thousands of designs obscured some of this history. Genuine horse brasses were always the property of the teamster, or plowman, not of the farmer who employed him, and sets of them were handed down from father to son. Here are some of the original designs.

The hex signs (hex means "witch" in German) on barn walls in certain parts of Pennsylvania are fairly recent. A whole industry to promote these designs has developed since they first appeared in the last quarter of the 19th century in south-eastern Berks county. Those interested in encouraging tourism in nearby areas have reproduced the designs in many forms, often in strange juxtaposition with pictures of the local Amish and Mennonites, who have always avoided any decoration on their buildings.

The symbols have ancient roots in the homeland of the German-Swiss settlers where for centuries they decorated books, furniture, and buildings. In this part of Pennsylvania some established farmers built very large barns. It is not surprising that familiar motifs were repeated on the large, blank walls, perhaps to enliven them. But when other farmers, liking what they saw, copied shapes from various Old Country mementos and frakturs, the controversy started. What did all those wheels, suns, and stars mean? They certainly reminded folk where they had come from and who they were in the New World. They were also extremely attractive and showed what someone could scratch out with large woodworking calipers on a surface that could be painted. If anyone remembered that these signs were originally for good luck and to keep away the unwelcome, so much the better.

Some typical hex designs from Pennsylvania.

Here we can see where modern hex bird signs come from. This fraktur is a baptismal certificate dating from 1815. Within the flower designs are other motifs that have been translated onto many barn walls.

Ten years earlier, the same artist decorated this certificate for five-year-old Benjamin Mayer. The six-pointed rosette is one of the most popular hex signs. The colored ink on both these illustrations was probably made locally from a limited range of earth pigments. By the time barn hex signs appeared, there was a wide choice of paint colors.

Country Graphics

The Goat & Compasses.

A pub in Hoosick, New York.

The village post office bulletin board is, in modern parlance, our network interface. All of local life is here: the news, bargains, help wanted, and jobs needed. This is what our valley was up to last winter.

The best job I never had was as a painter of English village pub signs. In my very early twenties, having been apprenticed as an artist, engraver, and calligrapher, loving history, and liking the refreshment that such establishments sold, I had a temporary fantasy of the perfect working life. I could have employed all my skills, studied the history of each pub, travelled the countryside, worked outside when it was fine, and illustrated each sign to please the innkeeper and locals. I was soon distracted, but what a great job idea.

When we look at pub signs, we can see symbols and illustrations doing the work of welcome in the same way they did when few people could read. Names like The Red Lion, The White Swan, The Ram's Head, The Golden Lamb, The Blue Dory, and The Black Friar swing in the breeze in areas all over America that were settled in the 17th and 18th centuries. The most common of the old names in both England and America is Red Lion, in France it's White Horse (*Cheval Blanc*), and in Germany, Golden Lion (*Goldener Lowe*) —all heraldic in origin. The most fun are those that have lost their original names after generations of distortion by the locals, especially in Britain. Here are a few: La Infanta de Castile became The Elephant and Castle, God Encompass Us became The Goat and Compasses, The Dorking Beacon became The Dog and Bacon, The Black Swan became The Mucky Duck. The Elephant's Nest and Blue Monkey defy explanation. Sadly, common names like The Bull and Bear date from times when some inns were places where these animals were baited by dogs for amusement.

The movable feast, and a declaration under way, at our local parade.

Appealing advertising, youthful charm, the honor system, and no preservatives.

Country Barn Raisings

In the happy event that you hear of a traditional barn raising, go to it. There will be lots to see and learn, and lots to do as well. You will certainly be well fed, but most importantly, you'll see how strangers are able to work together, have good evidence of it before sunset and, at the same time, become friends.

American farm buildings were well designed before nails and two-by-fours became the rule. The frames of barns, stables, and houses were pegged together and the main timbers were numbered, making them easy to take down and move elsewhere on the farm.

Today, it often means taking the timbers to a new location to rescue a building from decay and oblivion. That is what friends of mine do—they save and restore worthwhile farm buildings and give them a new life. Re-raising these wonderful structures today doesn't really require a crowd of willing helpers, happy to spend a day working outdoors; after all, a complete barn frame can be put up with a crane and a half-dozen workers. But, from experience, there is nothing like the satisfaction and fun of being part of a team raising a barn the old way.

Here is a look at some traditional barn raisings: the first passages are personal accounts of typical 19th-century raisings; the later excerpt describes a barn being put up in one day a few years ago on a friend's small farm.

19th Century Barn Raising

About 1845, Grandfather built the new barn. He hired men to prepare the frame. They hewed the big timbers until they were squared to the proper dimensions for the foundations, uprights and great beams to hold the roof. Then they were mortised at the end and the proper places to insert the cross pieces and braces. Lastly, the rafters and ridge-pole were cut and piled ready to be quickly used without confusion. Finally wooden pins were made to fasten the frame together.
From *Aroostook Pioneers* by Mary Elizabeth Rogers

When the hands arrived, the great beams and posts and joists and braces were carried to their place on the platform, and the first bent was put together and pinned by the oak pins that the boys brought. Then the pike poles were distributed, the men, fifteen or twenty of them, arranged in a line abreast of the bent; the boss carpenter steadied and guided the corner post and gave the word of command. 'Take holt, boys!' 'Now set her up!' 'He-o-he!' (heave all heave), 'he-o-he!' at the top of his voice, every man doing his best. Slowly the great timbers go up; louder grows the word of command, till the bent is up. Then it is plumbed and stay lathed, and

another is put together and raised in the same way, till they are all up. Then comes the putting on of the great plates, timbers that run lengthwise of the building and match the sills below. Then, the putting up of the rafters.
From *In the Catskills* by John Burroughs

As soon as the floor was laid, Bill and I set up plank tables and benches and the women brought pots of beans, brown bread, big roasts of veal and pork, a dozen pies and pitchers of cider. When Millie called, 'Victuals is ready,' there were thirty-eight hungry men washed up and ready to eat. Everyone was laughing and joking, and Millie and Annie ran back and forth between the table and the kitchen, bringing more pitchers of cider, tea, hot johnnycake, and more pie.
From *The Fields of Home* by Ralph Moody

. . . there was a dance on the big barn floor. On that ninety foot long floor the dancers had room aplenty to bow, circle, gallop and swing. The musicians, never more than three for such occasions, sat in the empty hayloft and played until two o'clock in the morning .
From *A Vanished World* by Anne Gertrude Sneller

Months of preparation preceded this day. The small forebay barn to be raised was first constructed before the middle of the 19th century by a man named Chamberline on a slope of his farm in Sand Brook, New Jersey. . . Beginning in late spring, the barn was carefully taken apart and trucked to the new site . . .

After an appropriate location was plotted, a substantial foundation for the barn was laid up in block and fieldstone. Next the timbers were repaired; in some cases replacement pieces were fashioned. The old sill and floor joist system was reassembled and a floor was laid. Framing members were inventoried and stocked in readiness around the site. The time had arrived for the raising . . .

With the gin pole in place, the raisers began assembling the first bent on the barn floor. Many hands were required to align the tenons with their corresponding mortises before the joints were finally closed with the beetle. . . . Those who assembled the sturdy oak frame could not help but appreciate the craftsmen of an earlier generation, who had skillfully cut the joints . . .

The strategy for raising the bents combined hoisting by hand with lifting with the block and tackle. At the direction of the boss carpenter to 'Heave ho!' some participants pulled the rope while others lifted together. The bent stirred, and rose slowly off the barn floor . . .

The barn raising took on a rhythm as periods of frenzy and excitement were interspersed with pauses for the relaxed preparation of the next state. Dogs ran in the field, musicians played, and many participants sat and talked and watched until the next call to raise a bent. . . .

Tired but happy, the members of the crew climbed down and stepped back to admire what they had accomplished. Silhouetted against the sunset, the barn frame looked noble and grandly serene. There had been no injuries other than a few souvenir splinters, though there would be some satisfyingly sore muscles the next day. In keeping with barn-raising tradition, a festive dinner was served. As the autumn chill returned to the air, a bonfire made of scraps of wood that had accumulated on the site lit the faces of the newly initiated, latter-day barn raisers. From *Barn* by Elric Endersby, Alexander Greenwood, and David Larkin

A Barn as a House

Friends of ours once lived in an historic farmhouse on a dead-end lane in the Kent countryside. Two hundred yards away, at the very end of the lane, was a fine old hip-roofed barn and a hop kiln, both threatened with demolition by the retired neighboring farmer, who wanted to develop the site. Since they valued their privacy highly, they decided to sell their lovely house and turn the two wrecks into a secluded new home.

It was an enormous project but, as has been said, location is everything. The old farmer told them the barn would be considerably warmer than their centuries-old farmhouse, which was sited on an earthen mound as protection against flooding. In contrast, the barn was built, its long side facing the sun, on lower ground where it received shelter from the prevailing winds.

The barn threatened with demolition.

The restored barn showing the large window that replaced the original entry.

132

At times our friends almost despaired because the restoration was slow and a great deal more expensive than they had calculated. To preserve the integrity of an old building you have to adapt to its structure, since too much change ruins or endangers the timbers. They did, however, have the luxury of all that extra space, and they were able to include favorite features from their former home. Later, the hop kiln was converted into a working studio and comfortable guest quarters. On my last visit, they were laying recycled red bricks to make a courtyard. Both enthusiastic gardeners, they are continually improving their corner of Kent according to the teachings of "Capability" Brown, the great 18th-century English landscaper.

The back garden of the new home. In the distance is the hop kiln with its new cowl.

The hop kiln before restoring . . .

and now as a guest cottage.

An old phone booth, rescued and now an outdoor shower.

Harvest and Celebrations

Harvest

Once ended thy harvest, let none be beguil'd,
please such as did help thee, man, woman, and child;
Thus doing, with alway, such help as they can,
thou winnest the praise of the labouring man.

From *Five Hundred Good Points of Husbandry* by
Thomas Tusser

Before the invention of the combine harvester, many hands were needed to cut and stack wheat before it was threshed and stored in the granary. As at the end of a successful barn or house raising, there were always feelings of pride and relief after a task well done—and a mood of celebration. It was thirsty work, and there was need for a "frolic" (from the Dutch *vroolijk*). On the next fine day, everyone would make a contribution by supplying the food, but it was the host who supplied the drink. The men and boys arranged competitive games involving feats of strength, balance, consumption of ale, and gumming (each contestant, head framed by a horse collar, tried to make the ugliest face). The women had competitions in quilting and spinning, but everyone joined in the singing and dancing. At one harvest event, two young ladies "spun a race" to determine who could lay claim to an eligible farmer. "*They began at six in the morning and spun until six in the evening. Two old ladies carded for them, one for each. At six o'clock Nancy was thirty rounds ahead. Forever afterward the fair Sarah had to look elsewhere for her swain.*"

From *Sugar Creek* by John Mack Faragher

The Old World harvest thanksgiving took place at the end of summer. The Puritans later moved it so that it would compete with Christmas. This lectern was used to read the lesson in the village church during the festival service. The European tradition of decorating altars and naves with farmers' produce and later giving it to the needy of the parish continues to this day. The book is Evelyn's *Silva*, my favorite source of information on timber and fruit trees.

In England also, the highlight of the farming year was the harvest. The men who cut the broad swathes up and down the field kept a lively pace. The farmer, knowing morale had to be high, sent out ale to refresh the workers. And when the last wagonload arrived home, the farmer would greet the workers with an invitation to a harvest dinner.

"And what a feast it was! Such a bustling in the farmhouse kitchen for days beforehand; such boiling of hams and roasting of sirloins; such a stacking of plum puddings, made by the Christmas recipe; such a tapping of eighteen-gallon casks and baking of plum loaves would astonish those accustomed to the appetites of today . . ."

From *The Village in England* by Graham Nicholson and Jane Fawcett

All over the world where grain is gathered, corn dollies symbolize the completed harvest and the hope of a successful one the following year. Their origins relate to beliefs that have been carried forward from the earliest days of cultivation. The names and shapes of these straw decorations, woven from wheat, rye, barley, or oats, change within countries and from country to country. The English "dolly" is thought to be a corruption over the centuries of "idol."

Suffolk horseshoes decorated the wagon carrying the last sheaves of wheat.

The Nek dolly, originally from Greece, became common in the west of England. The reapers made this from the last row of wheat or rye.

Countryman's favors were traditionally plaited by young men for their sweethearts' buttonholes.

The terret dolly comes from Essex in England. The design was based on the harness decoration that hung between the horse's ears.

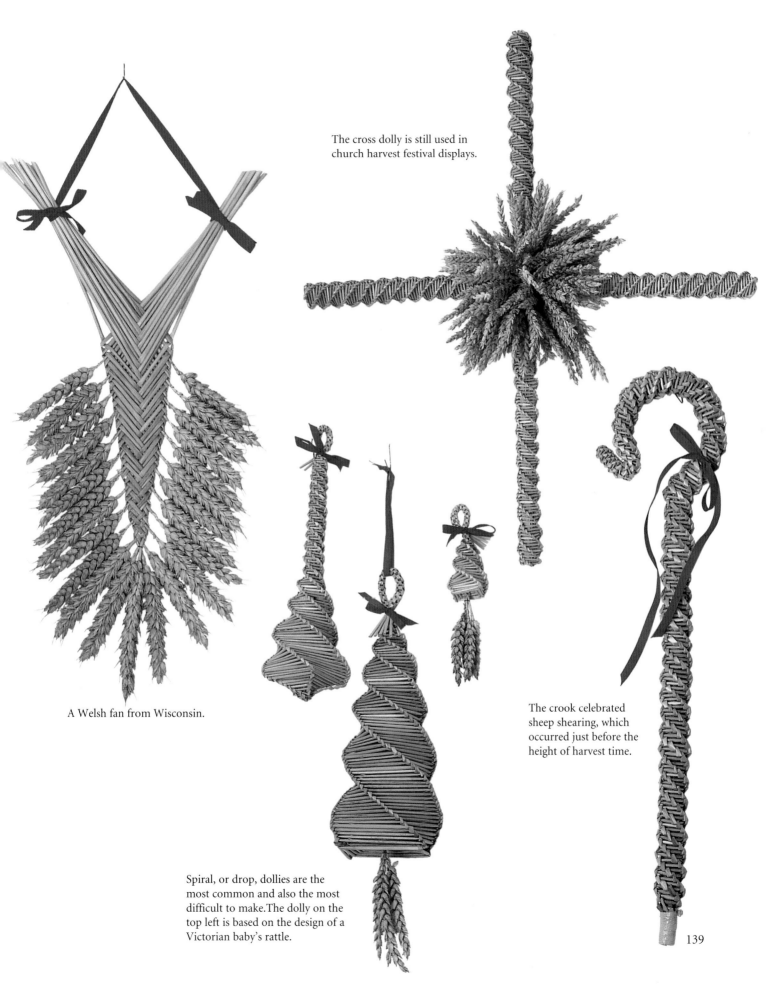

The cross dolly is still used in church harvest festival displays.

A Welsh fan from Wisconsin.

Spiral, or drop, dollies are the most common and also the most difficult to make. The dolly on the top left is based on the design of a Victorian baby's rattle.

The crook celebrated sheep shearing, which occurred just before the height of harvest time.

Celebrations

WEDDINGS

Blessed is the bride whom the sun shines on.

If you marry when the moon is getting fuller, you will prosper.

It is lucky to marry in a snowstorm.

If a bride wishes to be prosperous in her married life, she must wear something old, something new, something borrowed and something blue.

Wedding gowns:
Married in white,
you have chosen right;
Married in green,
ashamed to be seen;
Married in gray,
go far away;
Married in red,
wish yourself dead;
Married in blue,
love ever true;
Married in yellow,
ashamed of your fellow;
Married in black,
wish yourself back;
Married in pink,
of you he'll always think.

Wedding days:
Monday for health,
Tuesday for wealth,
Wednesday the best
day of all,
Thursday for losses,
Friday for crosses,
Saturday no day at all.

From the gathering of the harvest until the twelfth night after Christmas, there is an almost unbroken chain of get-togethers and celebrations. The communal relief that country folk experienced when they knew there was enough food to last them through the dark winter and beyond made harvest time the crown of the farming year. Even in the 20th century, sunburned workers stand among the golden stooks, joining in ceremonies they have always been part of, but hardly aware that such events have been going on since the days of ancient Egypt, Greece, and Rome. For example, before any celebratory feasts, harvesters treat the last uncut stalks with reverence, taking the best ears to fashion into idols, or corn dollies that were brought into the farmhouse and hung there for a year. It was considered bad luck to remove them until the next harvest, when they were taken outside and burned. Corn dollies also were made by haystack thatchers, who would set them on the top of completed stacks to show off the quality and quantity of their work.

In Christian times, depending on when the parish felt that all the grains, fruits, and vegetables were safely gathered in, the church held Sunday thanksgiving services. In Britain, where observance is close to the actual harvest, it is also a popular time for weddings. Here, a church is beautifully decked out with the season's abundance.

Scarecrows

The Shakers said they grew a little extra for the birds and rodents, but most food growers consider themselves to be at war with the wild creatures who eat their produce. Anyone who has worked hard plowing, fertilizing, planting, and watching over crops has a very unsentimental view of the opponent.

When fields were smaller, farmers had all sorts of devices and schemes to scare birds away. There were two main methods: the first was to use an effigy of some sort and the second was noise. A combination would be running out in the field and shouting. In fruit-growing areas, children with rattles were employed. Rural calm was shattered a few years ago by powerful electronic air horns used by some farmers. The public soon put a stop to them when they malfunctioned and went off at night like huge car alarms.

As for those lonely scarecrow figures in the garden or field, we never know quite what makes them effective— or not. Some, knocked together from plastic bags, pantyhose, and old buckets work brilliantly, while others, fully rigged and realistic, become perches and even nests. Anyway, they are lots of fun. My battleground is our raspberry patch. I have tried bird netting (they fly under) and a very realistic owl with staring eyes, just like those used on the roofs of baseball stadiums. When I see droppings on its head, I know I have more to do. There is another side to the scarecrow story, one that is a link to ancient times, when it was also known as a mawkin (from mannikin), hodmadod, and jackalent. A figure, often of straw, would be used to protect cattle, promote fertility, as a bogie to protect crops, and to scare more than birds. At the end of the season it would be offered in sacrifice to be consumed on the top of a bonfire, like Halloween effigies or the English Guy Fawkes figures in our own time.

But the clothes, in this case, were to be the making of the man. So the good woman took down from a peg an ancient plum-colored coat of London make, and with relics of embroidery on its seams, cuffs, pocket slaps, and button holes, but lamentably worn and faded, patched at the elbows, tattered at the skirts and threadbare all over . . . Next, came a pair of scarlet breeches . . .

Furthermore, Mother Rigby produced a pair of silk stockings and put them on the figure's legs, where they showed as unsubstantial as a dream, with the wooden reality of the two sticks making itself miserably apparent through the holes. Lastly, she put her dead husband's wig on the bare scalp of the pumpkin, and surmounted the whole with a dusty three-cornered hat, in which was stuck the longest tail feather of a rooster.

Nathaniel Hawthorne, using his knowledge of rural Massachusetts, describes a scarecrow in his short story, "Feathertop":

The most important item of all, probably, although it made so little show, was a certain broomstick, on which Mother Rigby has taken many an airy gallop at midnight, and which now served the scarecrow by way of a spinal column, or, as the unlearned phrase it, a backbone. One of its arms was a disabled flail which used to be wielded by Goodman Rigby, before his spouse worried him out of this troublesome world; the other, if I mistake not, was composed of the pudding stick from the woodpile. Its lungs, stomach, and other affairs of that kind were nothing better than a meal bag stuffed with straw. Thus we have made out the skeleton and entire corporation of the scarecrow, with the exception of its head; and this was admirably supplied by a somewhat withered and shriveled pumpkin, in which Mother Rigby cut two holes for the eyes, and a slit for the mouth, leaving a bluish-colored knob in the middle to pass for a nose. It was really a respectable face.

144

Country Superstitions

Long ago, coastal areas in the Old and New Worlds had more than their fair share of haunted sites. It was an effective way to protect a smuggling business from nosey people and excise men. Strange lights, for example, would appear on cliff tops to lure ships with their valuable cargo to run aground or hit unseen rocks. On land, if a stranger got too near he might be jumped from behind and his head thrust in a rabbit hole, and a stick driven into the ground between his legs to prevent him from backing out. This was a favorite stunt of smugglers, causing little injury to the victim and giving time for the smugglers to get away. In Appalachia, you could count on empty houses being haunted, back hollows full of haints, and woods infested with poisonous snakes and the plague—always in the spots where local whiskey was being distilled.

Superstitions

For good luck, sweep something into the house with a new broom, before you sweep something out.

It is bad luck to take an old broom to a new house.

Never buy a broom in May, for it sweeps all luck away.

Its bad luck to turn a strange cat away from the door

It is bad luck to make a new opening in an old house.

Leave a house by the same door through which you entered, or you will be unlucky.

If you rock the cradle empty, then you shall have babies plenty.

If your apron falls from your waist a new baby is on the way.

A pregnant woman should only look on beautiful things so that her child should likewise be born well-favored.

Newborns should be given three gifts: an egg to ensure plenty; silver to bring wealth; and salt for protection against enchantment.

If a baby is put in the first April shower, it will always be healthy.

A baby should be carried upstairs before downstairs so that it will rise in the world.

To change a baby's name after you have named it will cause it to have bad luck all of its life.

Holly was hung on the door at Christmas so that witches would stay outside counting berries.

A horseshoe hung over the door, right way up to keep in the goodness, will keep witches away.

Horse brasses hung over the fireplace are also a protection against witches.

Wood spitting in the fireplace was believed to be the Devil coming down the chimney.

Sneezing at the table is a sign of company at the next meal.

If you sneeze while something is being said it is the truth

If you dream of a river, it means that something stands between you and your wishes.

To dream of snakes brings bad luck.

If you eat black-eyed peas on New Year's Day, you will have good luck all the year.

A man must be the first person to cross your threshold on New Year's Day, or you will have bad luck throughout the coming year.

When starting a journey, throw salt over your right shoulder to ensure safety.

If you catch a falling leaf, you will have twelve months of happiness.

To find a rusty nail is good luck. The nail should not be picked up, but the ends should be reversed, so luck will come your way.

Stems of tea floating in the cup indicate strangers. The time of their arrival is determined by placing the stem on the back of one hand and smacking it with the other; the number of blows given before it is removed indicate the number of days before the stranger's arrival.

It is unlucky to eat a fish from the head downwards; secure good luck by eating the fish from the tail towards the head.

If a married man dreams that he is being married, it means that he is going to die.

If you bring an axe or hoe or spade into the house on your shoulder, a member of the family will die soon.

If a person dreams that he sees a naked figure dancing in the air, it means that death will come and release a soul from its body.

If rain falls on a coffin, it indicates that the soul of the departed has "arrived safe."

Never carry a corpse to church by a new road.

If a cock crows at midnight, the angel of death is passing over the house.

The howling of a dog is a sad sign. If repeated for three nights, the house will soon be in mourning.

After a person dies, cover all the mirrors in the house to prevent the soul being caught.

Hag stones—flints with holes in them—were at one time thought to be a safeguard against witches or evil, and were hung on stables and barns and under eaves of houses, or even carried in the pocket. And, if tied to the head of the bed, they would prevent nightmares.

Rocks, of natural formation, with an opening or hole through which a person could crawl were thought to promote cures for backache, rheumatism and other ills.

Jump across the doorsill when entering the house at night, so the spook cannot get hold of the heel left behind the other.

Glastonbury Tor in the distance has more legends and superstitions connected to it than any other place in Britain.

Some Grave Humor

The common gravestone probably originated as a flat slab, an effort to protect the corpse from wild beasts. In the Western world, it rose up first as a form of identification and then as the background of an epitaph, a pious inscription giving an opinionated view of the life of the deceased. Quotations offered advice and warnings from the grave. Early country epitaphs minced no words and used no soft expressions to veil the facts: sinners were sinners and saints were saints. Skulls are on the earliest stones but, gradually, sentiment began to appear. First, the skull got wings to fly to heaven, next the head was fleshed out a bit, a wig was added and then curls, and so on until a chubby cherub symbolizing everlasting peace and hope adorned many gravestones. The words, also, were under the control of the survivors, who often looked at the face of death and told it like it was, using vernacular puns, jokes, and insults. In today's light, there is some unconscious humor, too, in spelling mistakes, and in my favorites, Victorian moral encouragements. Like good stories, some epitaphs travelled far and were borrowed throughout the English-speaking world within a surprisingly short time.

Thank you sweet battle axe for 23 years of hell and happiness.
DELAWARE

He recommended himself very highly
DELAWARE

I told you I was sick.
DELAWARE

Here lies the body of Mrs. Mary,
wife of Dea. John Buel ESQ.
She died Nov. 4 1768 Aged 90
Having had 13 children
101 grand-children
274 great-grand-children
49 great-great-grand children
410 Total. 336 survived her.
CONNECTICUT

Soon ripe
Soon rotten
Soon gone
But not forgotten.
MASSACHUSETTS

Hail!
This stone marks the spot
Where a notorious sot
Doth lie:
Whether at rest or not
It matters not to you or I.
ENGLAND

Sacred to the memory of three twins.
VERMONT

Of children in all she bore twenty-four
Thank the Lord there will be no more.
ENGLAND

This is what I expected but not so soon
(age 21)
NEW YORK

Fair Maiden Lilliard
lies under this stone
Little was her stature,
but great was her fame.
Upon the English lions
she had laid many thumps,
And when her legs was cutted off,
she fought upon her stumps.
SCOTLAND

Here lies one Wood enclosed in wood,
One Wood within another.
The outer wood is very good,
We cannot praise the other.
MAINE

Gone to be a angle.
TENNESSEE

Under this pile of stones
Lie the remains of Mary Jones.
Her name was Lloyd, it was not Jones,
But Jones was put to rhyme with stones.
AUSTRALIA

This rose was sweet a while,
But now is odour vile.
NEW HAMPSHIRE

Sacred to the memory of
Anthony Drake,
Who died for peace and quietness sake;
His wife was constantly
scolding and scoffin',
So he looked for repose
in a twelve-dollar coffin.
MASSACHUSETTS

This disease you ne'er heard tell on —
I died of eating too much melon;
Be careful, then, all you that feed—
I Suffered because I was too greedy.
ENGLAND

We can but mourn our loss,
Though wretched was his life.
Death took him from the cross,
Erected by his wife.
MAINE

Here lies the body of
Thomas Vernon
The only surviving son
of Admiral Vernon
ENGLAND

Stranger call this not a place
Of fear and gloom,
To me it is a pleasant spot
It is my husband's tomb.
MASSACHUSETTS

She lived with her husband
fifty years
And died in the confident
hope of a better life.
VERMONT

Grieve not for me, my husband dear,
I am not dead, but sleepest here,
With patience wait, prepare to die,
And in a short time you'll come to I.
(added later)
I am not grieved my dearest life;
Sleep on, I have another wife;
Therefore, I cannot come to thee,
For I must go and live with she.
ENGLAND

My wife lies here.
All my tears cannot bring her back;
Therefore, I weep.
VERMONT

Halloween

Interest in Halloween is much stronger in the United States than in Europe, where it originated. An Irish import that seems to grow more popular here each year, it bridges the original harvest season and Thanksgiving. I love it, but my Irish forbears in Britain paid it little attention, and I don't remember being aware of Halloween during the two autumns I spent in Ireland. The timing is right, with that first real chill in the air and the leaves colored like flames. The clocks are just back an hour, so dusk arrives earlier. It seems a good occasion for something to happen.

The Celts thought of this time as the end of the old year. The spirits and souls of the dead would arise for one night before they could begin a new year. In Christian times, this night became All Hallows Eve, Hallowmass, or Night of the Dead. It was a time to pray against evil and tell stories about ghosts. Country folk would scare off these ghosts by pretending to be spirits themselves and lighting big bonfires for courage. The lads would get up to mischief, riding farmers' horses around at night to make them sweat as if they had been ridden by fairies, or stealing and putting the blame on witches. They also used the occasion to settle old scores, perhaps those originating at the other end of the year, May Day, when their romancing had been stopped by the father of a love interest.

Jack O'Lantern was an Irish ghost who carried glowing embers from hell in a large turnip hollowed out to make a lamp for his journey back to earth. Where we live, the bigger pumpkin makes a brighter lantern.

This group was carved by Tennessee schoolchildren.

Yuletide

The darkest part of the year is a good time to have a party. Before Christianity, people in the northern hemisphere knew that the winter solstice occurred when the night was longest, with the sun slowly returning to bring more light each day. With that in mind, exactly halfway through their winter gloom was a time for feasting. Ancient Romans celebrated Saturnus, the god of agriculture. Slaves were temporarily free, presents were exchanged, candles were lit, and evergreens were brought in to decorate the halls. The carnival, which means "finishing off" the meat, went on for days. Most scholars agree that Christians, for their own purposes, appropriated celebrations that had been going on for centuries. Beginning in medieval times, grain, nuts, fruit, and root crops from the harvest were carefully stored, and geese and swine were fattened for the winter feast.

Now the feasting, for the most part, begins on Christmas Eve and continues Christmas Day, and it evokes the traditions of all the people who settled America. As immigrant groups were folded into American culture, they gradually centered their celebrations around Christmas rather than St. Nicholas' Day, St. Lucia's Day, or Three Kings' Day, for example. However, each group prepared the symbolic and festive foods that had been traditional for centuries, often as far back as pagan times. Many of these delights take the form of sweets ranging from yeast breads, cakes, and pies to cookies, fritters, and puddings. Around Christmas, depending on where you live, you might be able to sample Mexican *buñuelos,* Italian *panettone,* German *stollen,* Swedish gingersnaps, English plum pudding with lucky coins, Puerto Rican *arroz con dulce,* or special breads from Czechoslovakia, Austria, Sweden, Finland, Greece, and most other European countries.

In America, because of the structure of communities, Christmas dinner seems to have no fixed time. In Germany it takes place at four o'clock on Christmas Eve, in France after midnight when the meal is ended with a chocolate Yule log, or *Bûche de Noël.* The British have their dinner in the early afternoon on Christmas Day, and get ready for parties with more food in the evening. The feast itself hardly ever changes. It has always been loaded with special treats, with hosts eager to show the amount of the harvest used for the celebration.

As Stephen Nissenbaum pointed out in his excellent book, *The Battle for Christmas,* all the trappings for the holiday were in place before the church got control—the bringing in of holly, ivy, laurel, mistletoe, and pine boughs to festoon the halls; the huge Yule log burning for days, a symbol that kept the merrymaking going until it turned to ashes; home-brewed wine and beer to be consumed with the precious roasted meat. This was the only time of the year that folk in the country, who had grown this feast, had anything really good to eat. Today, when most of us have plenty throughout the year, we have to think about how rare this occasion was—and still is—for all too many of us. The early colonists saw it as a time of indulgence, which they wished to avoid. They came to the New World to get away from excess, sure that Hugh Latimer, a 16th-century Anglican bishop, was right in saying: "Men dishonor Christ more in the twelve days of Christmas, than in all the twelve months besides."

The early part of the 17th century was an active time for the Puritans in England and the New World, who resolutely obtained religious and political control over their fellow citizens. The Puritan fathers were aware of the pagan connections to Christmas, and did not want the plain Christian holy days usurped by men and women who, in their opinion, just wanted to have a good time. So, in 1659, the Massachusetts Bay Colony outlawed Christmas as a public holiday. Anyone could be fined for feasting, drinking, or not working. The law was never totally successful, although it was nearly one hundred years before Christmas as a joyous festival recovered in New England.

Mince pies being prepared just before Christmas.

In the meantime, each ethnic group brought Christmas traditions to these shores, and today we have a happy mixture. For example, the Christmas tree, an old symbol of growth and light, was rediscovered in parts of Germany in the 18th century and established in Britain and America in the early 1800s. The singing of carols out-of-doors in the village square or at the front door follows from an ancient excuse to go wassailing (from the Anglo Saxon *Wes ha'l,* meaning "good health"). As many English children did, I knew a lot of carols and their verses. We would get a good number of carolers together to sing, like medieval wassailers, outside a house until someone opened the door and paid us to go away. The tradition of giving on Christmas Eve goes back to the Old Country: to Sweden where sheaves of grain were left outside for the birds, France where bread was given to the stable

animals, Poland where porridge was put out to keep Jack Frost away from the young crops, and Denmark where rice pudding, with a pink pig in it, was put in the attic for the elves. We can see how Santa Claus got his milk and cookies.

Another symbol—St. Nicholas, Kriss Kringle, Santa Claus, or Father Christmas—is still evolving. For this season, his invention as a distributor of gifts and an arbiter of good behavior in the young is convenient and worth preserving. Where did he come from? He is an icon with a costume different in each country where he is known. For example, in Holland, as St. Nicholas, he has a long gown, originates from the 4th century, and visits on December 6. All that is common today is the beard and the red clothing, a connection to his past as a bishop.

Holly

The holly and the ivy,
When they are both full grown,
Of all the trees that are in wood,
The holly bears the crown:
Old Christmas Carol

Holly, the common name for Ilex,
is a genus of decorative trees or
shrubs having beautiful, glossy
leaves and, usually, bright red berries.
Another Yuletide custom going back
centuries, holly, representing the male,
and ivy, the female, were hung in the
house to bring fortune and fertility.
They supposedly could enter the house
safely only on Christmas Eve, carried by a man.
An abundance of holly berries, in old
weather lore, was believed to
signal a cold winter ahead.

Mistletoe

Mistletoe is the common name for a large family of parasitic plants infesting the branches of various kinds of trees. It was gathered here in the United States for the Christmas holidays because it resembles the traditional mistletoe of Europe that for centuries has had Yuletide significance. It is said that mistletoe growing on oak branches made the tree sacred to the pre-Christian Druids, and was cut down with a golden knife to be used in rituals. It was hung as a sign of welcome. Kissing under the mistletoe, a custom that still survives today, was originally linked to midwinter fertility rites.

157

Conclusion

Most country wisdom has been passed down from generation to generation in the form of oral and written reminiscences, or from writers, poets, and those who just observed. Old country sayings, rituals, even superstitions stay with us because they haven't been proved ineffective. They are also worth preserving just for the fun they bring us. Certainly, many of the remedies really work, and some of their active ingredients are now manufactured for general consumption or application.

Apart from some observations on the weather, local life, and harvest festivities, our focus has remained inside the house. But there are other buildings on the property to think about, as well—fields, walls, fences, and gardens. And perhaps most interesting of all is the wild side of country living; what we can learn from, use, and live with nature without changing it.

It is hard to concentrate on just relaxing in the country. There is too much going on. Nature is very busy, so it's best to join in. Gardening, carpentry, walking around, and maintaining your property are creative, healthy, enjoyable, and, at the end of the day, relaxing. And, even more important, ways to a better life.

Bibliography

Baker, Ronald L. *Hoosier Folk Legends*. Bloomington:Indiana

Burroughs, John. *In the Catskills*. Boston: Houghton Mifflin, 1911.

Chambers, Dennis. *Haunted Pluckley*. Maidstone: Denela Enterprises, 1984.

Child, Mrs. *The American Frugal Housewife*. Boston: Carter, Hendee, and Co., 1833.

Coffin, Tristram P., and Hennig Cohen. *Folklore in America*. Garden City: Doubleday & Company Inc., 1966.

El-Hai, Jack. *Minnesota Collects*. St. Paul: Minnesota Historical Society, 1992

Endersby, Elric, Alexander Greenwood, and David Larkin. *Barn: The Art of a Working Building*. Boston: Houghton Mifflin Company, 1992.

Evans, George Ewart. *Ask the Fellows Who Cut the Hay*. London: Faber and Faber, 1961

Fapso, Richard J. *Norwegians in Wisconsin*. Madison: The State Historical Society of Wisconsin, 1982.

Faragher, John Mack. *Sugar Creek: Life on the Illinois Prairie*. New Haven: Yale University Press, 1986.

Garrett, Wendell. *American Colonial*. New York: The Monacelli Press, 1994.

Glassie, Henry. *Passing the Time*. Dublin: The O'Brien Press, 1982.

Habenstein, Robert W., and William M. Lamers. *The History of American Funeral Directing*. Milwaukee: Bulfin Printers, Inc., 1962.

Haining, Peter. *The Scarecrow*. London: Robert Hale Limited, 1988.

Hartley, Dorothy. *Lost Country Life*. London: Macdonald & Janes Publishers, Ltd., 1979.

Jackson, J.B. *The Necessity for Ruins*. Amherst: University of Press, 1980.

Knipping, Mark. *Finns in Wisconsin*. Madison: The State Historical Society of Wisconsin,1977.

Knipping, Mark. *Finns in Wisconsin*. Madison: The State Historical Society of Wisconsin, 1977.

Lampell, Ramona, and Millard Lampell. *O, Appalachia*. New York: Stewart, Tabori & Chang, 1989

Maynard, Samuel T. *The Small Country Place*. Philadelphia: J. B. Lippincott Company, 1908.

Mitchell, D.G. *My Farm of Edgwood: A Country Book*. New York: Charles Scribner, 1863.

Moody, Ralph. *The Fields of Home*. New York: Norton, 1953

Nicholson, Graham, and Jane Fawcett. *The Village in England*. New York: Rizzoli International Publications, Inc., 1988.

Nissenbaum, Stephen. *The Battle for Christmas*. New York: Alfred A. Knopf, 1996.

Noble, Allen G. *To Build in a New Land: Ethnic Landscapes in North America*. Baltimore: The Johns Hopkins Press, 1992.

_____. *Wood, Brick and Stone: Barns and Farm Structures*. Amherst: The University of Massachusetts Press, 1984.

Of Plates and Purlins: Grandpa Builds a Barn. Bethpage, N.Y.: Early Trades and Crafts Society and Friends of the Nassau County Museum, 1971.

Oliver, Edith. *Country Moods and Tenses*. London: B.T. Batsford, Ltd., 1941.

Roberts, Isaac Phillips. *The Farmstead*. New York: The Macmillan Company, 1902.

Rogers, Mary Elizabeth Barker. *Aroostook Pioneers*. Camden, Maine: Down East Magazine, 1968.

Sneller, Anne Gertrude. *A Vanished World*. Syracuse: Syracuse University Press, 1964.

Williams, Henry L., and Ottalie K. Williams. *How to Furnish Old American Houses*. New York: Farrar, Straus & Giroux, Inc.,1949.

Zeitlin, Richard, H. *Germans in Wisconsin*. Madison: The State Historical Society of Wisconsin, 1977.

Zube, Ervin H., ed. *Landscapes: Selected Writings of J.B. Jackson*. Amherst: University Massachusetts Press, 1970.

Acknowledgments

I would like to thank the following for their help in the preparation of this book:

Chris and Edna Bergstrom; Lois Brown; Tommy Candler and Alan Plaistow; Ronnie and Becky Dodd; Bill Duff; Elric Endersby and Alexander Greenwood; Edie Evans; Liza Fosburgh; Michael Freeman and Paul Rocheleau, creative photographer-authors, who put up with this preoccupation while we travelled thousands of miles together; the Galloway family of Mount Farm; John and Betty Holmes, East Enders and now East Anglians for over 20 years, for support and the gathering of information; Marc and Vivienne Jaffe for their editorial direction; Ian Ross Jenkins and Maria Carvainis; Colin Larkin; Ellen Larkin; Arthur and Jean Magri; Meredith Miller; John Owen; Roger Phillips; Elaine Rocheleau; Brian and Lizzie Sanders; Meg Schaefer; Bridget A. Scott.

Photo Credits

Tommy Candler, 41 *top*, 53, 66 *left and right*, 67 *bottom left*, 84, 113 *bottom*, 117 *top*, 127 *center left and right*, 127 *bottom right*, 132 *top and bottom*, 133 *top and bottom*, 138-139, 140, 141, 145, 152, 154

Bruce Coleman, Inc.: Adrian Davies, 117 *bottom*; Keith Gunnar, 117 *top*; Dotte Larsen, 112 *bottom*; C.C. Lockwood, 144 *left*; S. Nielsen 112 *center*; Masha Nordbye 112 *top*; Mike Price, 113 *top and bottom*; Bradley Simmons, 110; Steve Solum, 143; Gary Witney, 109

Gary Day-Ellison, 81

Michael Freeman, 6, 12-13, 13 *bottom right*, 14-15, 18-19, 25, *top and bottom right*, 28, 30-31, 31 *bottom right*, 32, 33, 34, 35, 56-57, 58, 62-63, 63 *right*, 64, 67 *top right*, 72, 73, 80 *bottom*, 96, 98, 102, 110, 114-115, 119, 120, 121, 122 *top*, 123, 146-147, 149

Robert Harding Picture Library, 8-9, 23, 78, 86, 116 top, 116 *center*, 116 *bottom*, 134-35, 155

Fred Hoogervorst, 42

Chuck KIdd, 129

David Larkin, 16, 22 top, 24, 27 *bottom right*, 41 *bottom right*, 80 *top*, 99, 100 *right*, 101 *top, bottom right and left*, 108, 126 *right*, 127 *top left and right*, 127 *bottom left*, 137, 144 *right*, 148, 150 *top*, 151, 158

Roger Phillips, 7, 156, 157

Paul Rocheleau, 2-3, 10, 11, 17, 20, 21, 22 *bottom*, 26-27, 36-37, 37 *bottom right*, 38, 39, 40, 44-45, 46-47. 48. 49, 50-51, 52, 54-55, 60, 61, 65, 68, 69, 71, 74-75, 76, 88, 90-91, 92, 93 *top right, bottom left and right*, 94 *top*, 94 *bottom*, 95 *top*, 100 *left*, 104-105, 106, 107, 118, 122 *bottom*, 125 *center bottom*, 126 *left center*, 127 *center*, 128, 130, 131, 136, 142, 150 *bottom*

Elizabeth Whiting Associates, 153